HOW TO
START MAKING MONEY
WITH YOUR CRAFTS

HOW TO
START
MAKING
MONEY
WITH YOUR

KATHRYN CAPUTO

BETTERWAY BOOKS
CINCINNATI, OHIO

To Peter who supported my creative efforts.

To Chrissy who believed in me.

And to Vada who was always there to help me.

How to Start Making Money With Your Crafts. Copyright © 1995
by Kathryn Caputo. Printed and bound in the United States of America.
All rights reserved. No part of this book may be reproduced in any
form or by any electronic or mechanical means including information
storage and retrieval systems without permission in writing from the
publisher, except by a reviewer, who may quote brief passages in a
review. Published by Betterway Books, an imprint of F&W
Publications, Inc., 1507 Dana Avenue, Cincinnati, Ohio 45207. (800)
289-0963. First edition.

Other fine Betterway Books are available from your local bookstore
or direct from the publisher.

99 98 97 96 95   5   4   3   2   1

Library of Congress Cataloging-in-Publication Data
Caputo, Kathryn
    How to start making money with your crafts / Kathryn Caputo.
        p.   cm.
    Includes index.
    ISBN 1-55870-400-0 (alk. paper)
    1. Handicraft industries—Management.   2. New business
enterprises—Management.   I. Title.
HD2341.C36   1995
745.5'068—dc20   95-24527
                                                          CIP

Edited by Greg Albert
Cover and interior designed by Angela Lennert
Illustrations on page 119, 122 and 124 by Cathryn Cunningham

Betterway Books are available at special discounts for sales promotions, premiums and fund-raising use. Special editions or book
excerpts can also be created to specification. For details contact:
Special Sales Manager, Betterway Books, 1507 Dana Avenue, Cincinnati, Ohio 45207.

Acknowledgments

First and foremost, my deepest appreciation to David Lewis for giving me the opportunity to write this book. Many thanks also to Greg Albert who patiently saw me through the editing of the original manuscript. Thanks also to Ann Royalty, Marilyn Daiker and all of the other creative minds at Betterway Books who had a hand in shaping this finished edition.

Special thanks to the many new crafters who asked the questions that I had the opportunity to answer in this book. I hope I answered them all. And, finally, my thanks to those veteran crafters and artisans who contributed their time, patience and advice to help me complete this work—particularly Carol Lebeaux, Roger Standt and Peter Stone.

About The Author

Kathryn Caputo lives in Bethel, Connecticut with her fifteen-year-old daughter, Chrissy. She has been an active crafter for more than ten years but didn't take crafting seriously until 1989 when she lost her full-time job.

Disenchanted with the corporate life, and not wanting to once again start at "the bottom of the ladder" or put her future into someone else's hands, Kathy turned to crafting as a full-time business. Finally, she could set her own business hours, be more available to meet her daughter's needs, and satisfy her own creative spirit—all from the comforts of her own home.

Participating in craft shows ultimately led to producing craft shows of her own. To date, Kathy has produced and promoted more than forty craft shows in her own and neighboring states. She has also produced shows for other industries.

Table of Contents

INTRODUCTION

Crafting can be a fun way to earn extra money in your spare time. It can also be a full-time business that lets you travel, meet new friends and make money at the same time. Crafting is an excellent business for:

- *Retirees*: Wondering what to do with your newfound free time? Crafting can offer you a wonderful sense of accomplishment and fulfillment.
- *Couples*: Couples can work as a team to create a finished product. It offers you a common interest and can provide you with extra "pocket money."
- *Single parents*: Raising children is expensive, especially if yours is a one-income family. The crafts business offers a second job that you can do at home.
- *Mothers*: You can do crafting while your little ones are asleep or out playing. You can be home for your children and still have an interest of your own.

As you can see, the crafts business is flexible—it can adapt to almost any lifestyle. As long as you have some spare time, it can work.

Creative genius is not a prerequisite for launching a successful crafts business. Self-discipline is. Many crafts require no artistic skills, and much can be learned by observing other crafters, practicing technique, reading craft magazines, and following a few simple rules.

This book takes a step-by-step approach to building your craft ideas into a successful business. There are no technical terms—only simple instruction and advice. It starts with the basics and explores many possibilities. Each chapter ends with a self-quiz or worksheet to help you identify your strengths and needs, and to guide you toward success in your new venture.

Chapter one gives a profile of the typical crafter. It shows you what it takes to be successful, and walks you through the practical considerations to think about before committing to one craft or another.

Chapter two explores the craft options available to you. Even if you have already chosen a craft, this chapter may give you some unique ideas for using your materials and technique. There also are lists of some suppliers of craft materials to get you started.

Chapter three offers suggestions to help you decide what products to make. It shows you how to successfully define a product line that has continuity and focus, and it helps you decide which criteria and formulas to use to build a successful and interesting product line.

But you aren't just making crafts for sheer pleasure. You want to make some money from your home business too. Tending to the business aspects is not difficult, it just takes a little organization. Chapter four gives an overview of the business end of crafting—opening a checking account, collecting sales tax, acquiring proper insurance coverage, learning what the IRS expects of you, and more.

Chapter five is more exciting—it explains how to make the best possible *profit* from your crafts. By making smart purchasing choices, you can significantly increase your profit margin. By setting up a production schedule, you can produce your inventory more efficiently. And by pricing your products reasonably yet competitively, you can reap the best rewards.

Chapter six explains the craft show process—how to get accepted at shows, what to bring to a show, and even what to wear to make your presentation more appealing.

Chapter seven explains selling at craft shows, from amateur shows to professional wholesale shows. It also provides suggestions on how to produce your own craft shows.

If you thought that selling at craft shows was your only option, chapter eight shows you how to have a thriving crafts business without ever participating in a show. It explores *other* selling options—from selling wholesale to producing your own mail-order catalog.

Using the information in this book should substantially reduce your learning curve and give you the necessary tools to make money from your crafts.

CHAPTER ONE

TAKING THE FIRST STEP

Many people new to the craft industry have grand ideas of making huge amounts of money with little effort. They have had fun making some lovely craft pieces for family and friends, so why not make more and sell them? If it were as easy as that, *everyone* would be doing it.

Being a successful crafter is not difficult. But it is not easy either. It takes time. And commitment. A successful crafter can expect to make from $300 to $1,000 (or more) per week. You must be ambitious and dedicated to make this kind of money. It won't just "fall in your lap." But if you make some sacrifices and work hard, you will be successful.

Choosing a Craft

Choosing the right craft is the first step to a successful crafts business. Choose a craft that incorporates one or more of your own interests—areas that you already know and enjoy.

Anything that interests you can be turned into a profitable and enjoyable home craft business. Consider your life experiences, your hobbies and your special interests—anything that inspires you—and put them to work for you.

The following will influence which crafts and products you choose:
- Your talents and interests

CAROL LEBEAUX—CHARMING PORTRAITS FROM PAPER

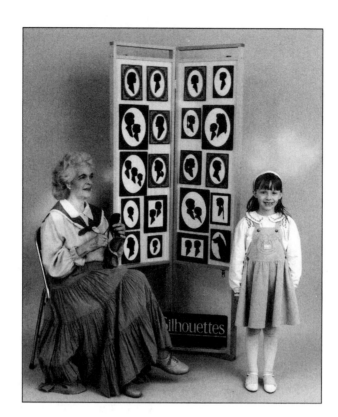

Carol Lebeaux is a very talented artist. Her first love is painting portraits in oil. But in today's busy world, not many subjects have time to pose at five or six long sittings. So Carol switched to making small portrait silhouettes. Making the silhouettes is a more portable form of art than oil portraits and Carol found her niche at craft shows, festivals and large county fairs.

These fine silhouettes are produced by cutting the subject's profile out of black paper and mounting the finished portrait in a frame against a light background.

Carol has combined art skills with craft skills to produce a more readily saleable product. The silhouettes take only about ten minutes each to make and they are done "on the spot." They are sold nicely framed, which makes for a lovely finished product package. The raw material costs are not expensive and Carol has no storage problem since her products are sold right after they are made.

Many of Carol's customers are also repeat business. Many of her subjects are children, and parents and grandparents return year after year to get new silhouettes of their little ones. Carol notifies prior customers when she is doing a show in their area.

Carol has a wonderfully focused product line. Her display is simple but very effective. And being able to demonstrate a craft at a show generates a great deal of interest—and sales!

- The time you can devote to your crafts
- The space you will need to make and store your products
- Safety precautions and equipment you need to produce your type of craft
- The transportation you will use to take your crafts to market

Your Talents and Interests

Let's take a look at your most important resource—*you*! Can you draw? Can you paint? If you can, maybe you would enjoy embellishing an already made product rather than producing a product from scratch and then painting or decorating it. You could paint country designs on precut wood, floral or herb designs on watering cans or flower pots or garden accessories, children's designs on small furniture pieces, primitive motifs on antique (or new) furniture or on wall plaques or clothing.

Can you sew? Perhaps you could design a line of clothing, or maybe just your own design of vests or beachwear. How about making a ''signature'' line of accessories: handbags, totes or other items? Or you might choose to make coordinated home accessories: tablecloths, napkins, table runners, decorative towels, bed linens, etc.

Do you collect dolls? Consider specializing in doll clothing or matching clothing for children and dolls.

Do you know a lot about flowers or herbs or vegetables? You might want to make floral arrangements or miniature herb paintings or herb wreaths or garden markers.

Do you have children? You might want to target a specific age group and make toys, games, wall plaques or accessories.

If you prefer working with small objects and creating detailed work, making miniatures or quilling might interest you. Larger scale items such as furniture, cabinets and quilts can also be successful product lines.

Maybe there is some craft you have always wanted to try. Now is the time to experiment and zoom in on your creative self. Take a pottery or ceramics class, or learn how to crochet or knit.

If you still can't think of any talents or knowledge that you can turn into a profitable crafts business, don't worry. These chapters list many interesting suggestions and ideas.

Time Management

Time management is an important part of any home business. And self-discipline is an important part of time management. Be prepared to schedule work time for yourself and stick to it. But remember, it is *your* schedule and you can plan it any way you like. Set aside specific time each day, or on specific days, to work on your crafts. If your children are at school during the day or take naps, plan to reserve blocks of time during those hours. If you work, set an evening schedule. If weekdays are already too hectic, schedule your craft hours on the weekend. (Just remember that if you plan to participate in craft shows, some of your weekend time will eventually be devoted to these shows.)

In the beginning, you may use this time to research your craft options, read craft magazines, go to the library, or just experiment with designs or craft techniques. Later, you can use this time for production and new product development. Try to make each session at least two hours long. You'll probably find that it takes at least half an hour just to get organized and into "crafting mode."

As you consider the many different crafts from which you can choose, also consider the *time* you have. For example, if you only have small periods of time, don't choose a craft such as quilting that will take hours and hours of work before you have a finished product. How long will it take before you have a good supply of quilts in a variety of patterns and color combinations? Probably a long time if you are a new quilter.

If your time is very limited, you might consider embellishing premade products. Not all crafters make their products from scratch. Some paint on old watering cans and saws; others appliqué or screen print sweatshirts and other clothing items; and still others buy their pottery already fired and only *paint* it themselves.

Crafting should be fun. Don't take on more than you can comfortably handle, especially in the beginning. Don't set so stringent a work schedule that it becomes stressful and too much of a "job." You will still get where you want to go if you take it slowly—it just might take you a little longer. That's OK. You will enjoy the journey much more and it will still be fun when you get to your destination.

Work Space

Space is an important factor to consider when choosing a craft that you will produce at home. You will need space to store your raw materials, to produce your product, and to store your finished pieces. If you have a limited area in which to work, choose a craft involving miniatures or jewelry rather than large furniture pieces!

Do you have a separate room in your home that can be dedicated to your new business? If not, can you turn a corner of your home or apartment into a "work station"?

Wherever you plan to set up your crafting, make it a permanent spot where you can keep your raw materials and produce your product. If you have to keep putting away and taking out your materials, you will be less likely to consistently produce. Also, having unfinished products always in view will help motivate you to sit down and get to work. Craft books will beckon you to read them if they are placed where you can see them.

Inventory takes up a lot of space, but you should keep your inventory together as much as possible. If it is scattered throughout your house, you won't be able to keep track of it. One Easter I made a whole product line of bunnies, fuzzy chicks and decorated eggs. They were adorable! After the last Easter show of the year, I put the remaining stock in a safe place. *So* safe that I couldn't find it until two weeks after the following Easter. The moral of the story is *do* keep all of your eggs in one basket, but remember where you put the basket!

Safety

Many new crafters do not realize the potential hazards of materials they work with or equipment they use. Look out not only for your safety but for the safety of your children and other family members. Crafting will be safer and lots more fun if you are careful.

Here is a safety checklist to protect you and your family:

- Read all label warnings and instructions carefully before using any product.
- Have adequate ventilation when using materials that give off harmful fumes.
- Wear rubber gloves when working with chemicals or chemical dye solutions.
- Use a dust mask or air-purifying respirator when handling powders.
- Wear ear muffs or ear plugs when using loud equipment.
- Make sure tool guards are in place before operating equipment.
- Don't operate equipment when there are distractions.
- Never use potentially dangerous equipment when you are tired.
- Always give equipment your full attention and respect.
- Unplug all electrical equipment when it's not in use.
- Never leave equipment turned on and unattended.

Even a glue gun or electric scissors can present some hazards. Never leave them plugged in and unattended. Use low-temp glue with a low-temp glue gun. High-temp glue can cause serious burns—I have the scars to prove it! In fact, when I was at a craft show once, some of us crafters compared "glue gun scars" to see who had the "best" scars from hot guns and dripping hot glue. (Fortunately, I didn't win.)

Safety should also be a factor in deciding what products to make. Your products should be safe for their intended market. Dolls with eyes or small accessories that can be removed and possibly swallowed should not be sold for use by small children. A warning should be clearly stated on the packaging of any product that is potentially dangerous—even through misuse. I strongly suggest that you stay away from such potentially dangerous toys as slingshots and rubber-band guns. In my opinion, selling these types of products is irresponsible.

Transportation

If you plan to sell your merchandise at craft shows or to local stores, how will you get your products to market? Car space is gobbled up quickly once you start filling it with boxes, displays and product. As you acquire larger and more sophisticated display equipment and produce more inventory, always keep in mind that these items will have to fit in your car. Don't make your racks or shelving units eight feet high unless your vehicle can accommodate them.

Also consider who will be loading and unloading that car. If your products are heavy, can you manage them yourself? If you will require racks, tables, lattice or shelving to display your products at shows, make sure they are made of reasonably light materials and are as compact as possible.

And, finally, consider this: The only inventory you can sell is the inventory that you bring to the show. The more you can bring, the more you have a chance of selling. You can't make $500 in sales at a craft show if your car can only hold $350 worth of inventory. No matter how many ways you look at it, $350 in inventory can only be translated into a maximum of $350 in sales.

If you are considering buying a new vehicle or trading in your old one, think about getting something a little larger or one that's designed with a larger storage area—a bigger trunk or backseat.

The car you drive now might do just fine if your products are of average size. For years I drove to craft shows in a Pontiac Firebird. Each time I used it for a show, I learned to pack it a little better. At one show, one of my fellow crafters looked at my car, then looked at my display and inventory, laughed and shook his head. He didn't think all that stuff could have come out of that car. But it did. We crafters are a creative bunch—and this extends to creatively packing our vehicles.

Involving Your Family

When I first decided to make crafts at home, I overlooked many things. Like how my family would be inconvenienced. These were not major inconveniences, but you know how it is, sometimes *any* change can meet with initial resistance.

It seemed to them that overnight our home had been turned into a factory. Fabric was everywhere. The roll of batting I purchased was eighty inches high and bigger around than most people. There was no place to inconspicuously store it. This pillar of white fluff was a very obvious reminder that things were changing around my house.

Bare walls were decorated with wooden racks and dowels for hanging my fabric, trims and finished products. It was no longer the same comfortable home where you could walk around barefoot and relax. Straight pins, no matter how hard you try to avoid it, can get lodged in the carpet—and eventually in bare feet.

Now when I am in "production mode," I place a sign on the door that reads "Warning: Tree skirts at large. Pass at your own risk and wear shoes." And the sign works. After they got stuck by a pin once or twice, my family took it (and me) seriously.

The more you involve your family in your crafting, the less resistance you will encounter. The trick is not to create competition but to create harmony. If you are the family cook, try not to be late with dinner because you are crafting. Inconvenience your family as little as possible, especially in the beginning. Don't create a situation that leads to competition between your family and your crafts. You can successfully accommodate both with a little planning.

Once you have shown a little profit from your business, their attitude will change. But in the beginning, be patient with them. They do need some time to get used to the idea.

Try to involve them. Ask for advice. Even though you may not use it, it will involve them in your creative process. You never know—they may give you some valuable insight! Older children may enjoy participating in craft shows with you, and may even become accomplished salespeople. But, I don't recommend bringing small children to a craft show with you if you plan to make any money. You can't possibly watch them and talk to customers at the same time. It is a frustrating experience for both parent and child. If at all possible, try to find someone to watch your younger children at home.

Involving your family can make the whole process so much easier and more fun. Try it!

Originality

Don't copy another crafter's work. Some crafters have "licensed" their original work; copying it may lead to a lawsuit—think up your own new ways to use the different mediums. Let your own creativity shine through. Give yourself a chance to explore your own hidden talents.

Your product should be as original as possible. Even a traditional flower arrangement can have something special about it that says that it was made by *you*. Maybe the design is slightly different from others. Perhaps the colors are unique. Maybe the flowers are not the traditional ones that you would see in an arrangement. Your product should bear your "signature." Your ultimate goal is for people to recognize your work, and buy it.

Quality

Just because a product is handmade doesn't mean that it has to look homemade. The quality level at craft shows has increased significantly over the past decade. Your products will be sold in a very competitive marketplace and they need to be the best you are capable of making. Your sales and profits will be in direct proportion to the quality of your finished product.

Strive to make a product that is "store quality." Step back and objectively critique each product. Can you envision it being sold in a store? Would *you* buy it? Is it neat— no threads visible, no glue dripping, clean edges? Years ago, a little exposed glue here and there or a few threads out of place were acceptable. Not in today's marketplace. Refined customer tastes and an emphasis on the best possible product for the best possible price have changed all that.

Experiment!

There are many mediums and crafts from which to choose. You should experiment with many before deciding on one. Don't always "stick to the book" either. Follow the instructions, but don't be afraid to try your own variations. If you have an idea, go with it. Though it may not work out, it may give you new insights or lead to other ideas you would have otherwise missed. That's half the fun of crafting. *Play* with it!

You may already have a good idea of what type of products you will make. You may have already decided on the medium and craft technique that you will use. That's fine. It puts you way ahead of the game. But things can change, so be flexible.

Perhaps your original idea won't test well when you try to sell it. Maybe you'll find that the raw materials are too expensive and you can't make a decent profit on your original ideas. Be ready to regroup and try again. Say to yourself "I can do this" and try to analyze objectively why it didn't work. Make some adjustments and try again.

The next chapter offers suggestions on some of the major craft and medium categories. This is by no means a total list. At every craft show, I see a craft, technique or product that I have never seen before. This is good old American ingenuity at work.

MOP DOLLS

I created these two dolls to complement my Christmas theme product line. Many wonderful craft items have been made from unconventional materials. I initially arrived at the Santa design by mistake. The face was incorrectly painted (due to my lack of art skills) and I used the hair to cover up the error. The new design was so well received by customers, that I replaced my original design with the new one.

CHAPTER WORKSHEET

This short quiz will help you think about the many aspects of turning your craft activity into a moneymaking one. Clear thinking about these important considerations will get you off to a good start. Don't be discouraged if you answer NO to many of the following questions—use your responses to identify those areas to which you need to give special attention.

Time

Ask yourself "When will I have time to dedicate to making my crafts?"

Example:

| When the kids are at school | Noon—3 PM |
| In the evenings after work and after dinner | 8 PM—11 PM |

My projected schedule:

Day of the Week	Time of Day	Total Hours
Monday	_____	_____
Tuesday	_____	_____
Wednesday	_____	_____
Thursday	_____	_____
Friday	_____	_____
Saturday	_____	_____
Sunday	_____	_____
Total Hours per Week:		_____

Space

Do I have an area where I can store my supplies?	Yes	No
Is that area ever damp?	Yes	No
Should I consider buying a storage unit and putting it _____ (where)?	Yes	No
Do I have an area to accommodate my raw materials?	Yes	No
Is there a permanent location where I can set up my "workstation"?	Yes	No
Is it out of the way of family traffic?	Yes	No
Is there enough room for making what I want to make?	Yes	No

Are there one or more electrical outlets, should I need them?	Yes	No
Do I have a place where I can store my finished products?	Yes	No

Transportation

Can I fit 50 to 100 pieces of my product in my car?	Yes	No
Even if I add one or two tables or other display equipment?	Yes	No

Safety

Am I planning to use potentially dangerous equipment?	Yes	No
Is there adequate ventilation in my work area?	Yes	No
Do I need to purchase any safety devices? (window fan, rubber gloves, air filters, masks, etc.)	Yes	No
Can a product I plan to make be hazardous in any way?	Yes	No
Can I redesign it to make it less potentially hazardous?	Yes	No

CHAPTER TWO

EXPLORING YOUR CRAFT OPTIONS

Exploring your craft options and choosing a craft are by no means small tasks. First explore what you already know. Basing your crafts business on something you know will greatly reduce your learning curve and move you forward more quickly. If you're starting from scratch, you may be overwhelmed at first by all the choices. Take your time choosing. You want to make the right choices since you will probably be making these products and using your chosen craft technique for a very long time.

This chapter contains many suggestions and ideas for crafts. Some you have already seen, others you may have never heard of. Read with an open mind.

The object is to choose a craft—and products from that craft—that you will enjoy making and that people will want to buy.

Learning a new craft or perfecting one that you already know is half the fun! You will feel a unique sense of accomplishment when you master that particularly difficult stitch, that intricate pattern, that elaborate design.

You can find specific how to's for any craft in books and magazines at your local library, craft center or bookstore. Most have easy to understand step-by-step instructions. If you see a particular technique or craft listed in this book that you aren't familiar with, browse through a book on the craft to see if it might interest you.

You may also want to take a training class or course. Check your local craft centers, craft supply stores, and high school and college community education programs.

Some new crafters apprentice with an established craftsperson to learn a particularly intricate or difficult "trade." I suggest some hands-on experience and instruction before tackling any craft that requires expensive supplies.

Competition is keen, so whatever craft you choose, take the time to learn it well, and make each piece as if you were going to give it as a gift. Experiment with several crafts and products before you make a final decision. To better gauge your market potential, you might produce a small "test" product line, then try to sell your products at a church or school fair, at work or to friends. Be especially careful not to load up on raw materials for a craft until you're sure you like it and that it is likely to sell.

At the end of this chapter is a list of materials and equipment suppliers for many of the crafts listed here. Though no one company sells supplies for *all* crafts, there is one that stands out and deserves to be mentioned. Dick Blick Art Materials puts out a wonderful catalog that is by no means limited to art supplies. It contains information, instruction books and videos, raw materials and equipment for a wide variety of crafts and craft techniques. To order their catalog, call (800) 447-8192. I also recommend that you get a copy of *The Craft Supply Sourcebook* by Margaret A. Boyd, published by Betterway Books. It is a complete source guide for just about every craft imaginable.

Don't be afraid to experiment. New crafts and innovative ways to use old materials are being discovered every day. *You* may be the one to come up with that very special new product or idea.

Wood

Customers see value in wood items because wood is durable, solid and substantial. Wood lends itself to a number of techniques. It can be cut with a saw, carved with a knife or chisel, or turned on a lathe. Wood items can have designs that are burned, stained, stenciled, painted or decoupaged.

Woodworking is an especially good "couples" craft. One designs the patterns, the other cuts the wood, and one or the other can paint, stain or decorate it. Remember, "wood" does not only mean *hard* wood (oak, mahogany, rosewood, chestnut, maple, walnut, ash, butternut, elm, cherry, beech and locust). Many products can be made from balsa and other *soft* woods, such as pine, hemlock, cypress, redwood, spruce, poplar, bass, fir, cedar and larch. And don't discount "exotic" woods, such as teak, satinwood and rosewood. They may be more expensive to work with, but they are also a bit more "special."

You could make:

Furniture	Trays	Whirligigs
Towel Racks	Trains	Toy Chests
Picture Frames	Mosaics	Bookends
Paperweights	Buttons	Wagons
Lawn Furniture	Magazine Racks	Centerpieces
Coat Racks	Musical Instruments	Key Holders
Magnets	Cabinets	Marionettes
Figurines	Clocks	Napkin Holders
Tape Holders	Chairs	Flower Pots
Garden Markers	Jewelry	Birdhouses
Mailboxes	Buckles	Dollhouses
Puzzles	Trivets	Planters
Decoys	Boats	Coasters
Spoons	Cars	Cutting Boards
Shelves	Baskets	Airplanes
Tables	Desks	Board Games
Benches	Wall Plaques	Step Ladders
Signs	Doll Furniture	Rolling Pins
Bowls	Jewelry Boxes	Yo-yos

Desk Accessories—paperweights, pen holders, pen casings, letter openers, name plates
School Accessories—pencil boxes, rulers, etc.
Kitchen Accessories—rolling pins, spatulas, spoons, knife and kitchen tool caddies.

Be unique in your approach to wood. Many crafters out there are already selling wood shelves. Why not make all of your wood shelves corner pieces instead of straight wall shelves. You could also make corner cabinets, corner bookcases, corner hutches, corner tables, even corner chairs! Your whole product line theme could be wood corner pieces—a very unique and serviceable idea.

Not all woodworkers use new wood. Some have created whole product lines of driftwood pieces or have incorporated driftwood and other "found" wood into their products.

Floral

Floral designs are always well received, but the market is saturated with floral vendors. If you like to create florals, look for something different! You could use dried flowers,

CAROL ROTHSTEIN— FLORALS

Carol Rothstein began her crafts career when she was laid off from her job. She had always loved flowers and had a lovely flower garden at her home, so it seemed only natural to Carol that she expand her knowledge of flowers and design to create a successful floral design business.

Carol took one continuing education course in floral design and "read lots of books" on gardening, flowers and floral arrangements, drying flowers and herbs. Carol experimented with growing and drying her own florals so she could control the age of the dried flowers that she used in her own arrangements and her potpourri. She also researched other suppliers for florals that she couldn't grow herself because of climate and space restrictions. Carol researched sources and practiced her drying and arranging techniques for two years before she participated in her first craft show.

Of her first show, she says, "My display was awful—I hate to even think about it! I actually used a vinyl table cover! I was amazed that anybody would even buy my stuff!" But they did. At her first show, she made $400. At her first Christmas show, she grossed $1,000 and she was hooked. Now Carol says that she "dreams flowers."

Her advice for new crafters: Have a nice set-up, watch your pricing and target your market.

silk flowers, or dried-look silk flowers, but why not make your own original flowers and leaves from fabric, clay, bread dough, leather, wood, ribbon, stained glass, paper, corn husks, yarn, papier-mâché or metal? Or make your designs from wheat, pretty weeds, leaves, herbs or wildflowers.

I was at a craft show where one of the vendors made lovely stemmed roses from dried apple slices. How unique! And they sold very well. Another crafter named Ann makes roses and rosebuds from bread dough. They are lovely!

You could make:

Hair Accessories	Potpourri	Centerpieces
Wedding Accessories	Wall Decorations	Hanging Baskets
Arrangements	Wreaths	Topiary Trees
Bouquets	Magnets	

Fabric

Now here's another category with endless possibilities! Look around at all the different items that can be made with fabric. You can dye, stencil, knit, appliqué, quilt, embroider, smock, batik and tie-dye many different types of fabric! Cotton and cotton blends are not the only fabrics available. Don't forget such unconventional fabrics as tapestry, canvas, duc, vinyl, terry cloth, nylon and silk!

You could make:

Wall Hangings	Handbags	Napkins
Tote Bags	Stuffed Animals	Appliance Covers
Wall Fans	Pillows	Wreaths
Duffle Bags	Rugs	Dolls
Table Linens	Pot Holders	Magnets
Doll Clothing	Jewelry	Baskets
Flags	Lamp Shades	Chair Pads
Curtains	Comforters	Quilts
Pillowcases	Kitchen Towels	Oven Mitts
Casserole "Cozies"	Hand Towels	Shower Curtains
Wastebasket Covers	Covered Mirror Frames	

You could also make:

Tapestry pillows or table runners

Canvas boat covers, golf bags and totes

Terry cloth seat covers, oven mitts and potholders

Vinyl mailbox covers

Apple Slice Roses

You can make very lovely and original flower arrangements without using real flowers. I made this rose out of apple slices.

Clothing and Accessories

Stay away from the all-too-common white T-shirts and sweatshirts. Even with unique designs, they have been seriously overworked. If you want to embellish a premade piece of clothing, look for a type of garment that you don't see sold anywhere else, something that you like and that you think your customers will like, something service-able. Be careful with sizing. A one-size-fits-most product will save you from making products in a large variety of sizes that may not all sell.

You could make:

Adult Aprons	Pet Clothing	Children's Rompers
Hats	Vests	Shirts
Ties	Dresses	Beach Cover-ups
Children's Aprons	Costumes	Jackets
Blouses	Sneakers	

How about:

Silk ties and pocket hankies

Canvas handbags

Vinyl raingear

Terry cloth beach cover-ups and hats

Tapestry vests

Men's clothing items and accessories are always overlooked. Though not too many men frequent craft shows, their wives, sisters, mothers and daughters do. And they shop for the men in their lives.

Patchwork, Quilting and Appliqué

Patchwork is the art of sewing different pieces of cut fabric together in a geometric (or other) pattern to form a mosaic.

Quilting is the technique of layering three pieces of cloth—the top layer has a design, the second layer is a "filler," and the final layer is the backing—and sewing through all three layers. The fabrics may be either hand- or machine-stitched together.

Here are some basic things to remember when choosing patchwork and quilt fabric:

- Cottons and cotton-blends work best.
- Choose fabrics that don't stretch or fray and that are not too "slippery."
- Combine materials with the same basic thickness and weight.
- Don't use old and new fabrics together in the same piece—they wear differently.

Appliqué is the art of applying pieces of fabric to a backgound cloth to create a picture or design. The three-dimensional effect can be enhanced by stuffing the design with poly-fill or batting. Appliqué is typically used to enhance sweatshirts and to make banners, flags or wall hangings.

The three techniques—patchwork, quilting and appliqué—are often combined in one item. For example, a quilt may contain patchwork squares with appliquéd designs on them. One precaution: Make sure that all the fabrics used in the same piece have compatible cleaning instructions.

You could make:

Bed Coverings	Pot Holders	Christmas Stockings
Table Runners	Pillows	Kitchen Accessories
Appliance Covers	Wall Hangings	Sweatshirts
Handbags	Vests	

Appliqué

This appliqué train is one of the motifs I use in my fabric designs. The appliqué has been stuffed with batting to raise it from the fabric and has been further embellished with sequins, braid and seed pearls.

Yarn and Thread

There are so many interesting things to do with yarns and threads. The variety of colors, textures, patterns and techniques make the possibilities exciting!

You can crochet, knit, embroider, needlepoint, cross-stitch or do crewelwork, tatting or smocking. You can make original items or embellish premade items, such as towels, tablecloths and pillows.

You can make:

Afghans	Scarves	Coats
Slippers	Pet Clothing	Leg Warmers
Shawls	Hats	Jackets
Pot Holders	Baby Items	Vests
Sweaters	Doilies	Table Runners
Doll Clothing	Gloves	Socks
Rugs	Headbands	Handbags
Table Linens	Clock Faces	Coasters
Pillows	Tote Bags	Seat Covers

You could also edge or decorate table and bath linens with crochet.

Paper

Paper crafts are fun to learn. You might even involve your children in this one! This is not to say that all paper crafts are easy—many require intricate technique for professional results. But some basic designs can be learned by almost anyone who takes the time to learn them.

Quilling

Quilling is very decorative and gives the finished product a lacy appearance. Thin strips of quilling paper are rolled, curled and pressed into designs. The rolled and pressed strips of paper are glued to a background or to each other. Floral designs are popular quilling motifs, but I have seen lovely patchwork quilt patterns replicated in quilled wall plaques.

Quilling can be used to create lovely earrings, framed designs and scenes, coasters, picture frames and glass-domed paperweights.

Origami

This Oriental art form consists of folding paper into three-dimensional shapes such as animals, people, plants, flowers and abstract designs. Typical origami paper is six inches square and colored on only one side, which makes a very striking finished product. The focus is on technique and intricate designs. Popular designs are swans, dragons, frogs, horses, dogs, birds, flowers, and lots of other subjects.

You can make:
Christmas Ornaments
Crib Mobiles
Whimsical Creatures
Paper Airplanes
Floral Arrangements
Earrings

Papier-Mâché

Papier-mâché is a "mash" of torn or shredded paper mixed with binding agents such as water, glue or epoxy. The mixture is applied to a predesigned form or mold. The objects are sometimes sanded and usually painted. There are also compounds that can be added to make your papier-mâché pieces waterproof and fireproof!

Papier-mâché is great for making earrings, figurines, piñatas, masks, decorative bowls, napkin rings and whimsical characters.

Silhouette Art

This is the art of cutting a silhouette out of black paper and applying it to a white background. This takes some talent. Not everyone is capable of cutting out someone's profile freehand. Usually, the finished product is framed. Silhouette cutting is very entertaining to watch at a craft show and usually draws a crowd.

If you are not confident enough to do on-the-spot portraits, you might try framed precut silhouettes of cats, dogs, scenes or skylines using ideas from magazines, cartoons, etc.

Silhouette Art

This silhouette was cut by Carol Lebeaux and is a portrait of my daughter, Chrissy.

Basketry

Basketry is a wonderful craft that always draws attention when demonstrated at a craft show. Research some interesting patterns—there are many from which to choose.

HOW TO START MAKING MONEY WITH YOUR CRAFTS

You can use reed, cane, rush, grass, corn husk, rope, raffia, cord, yarn, sisal, linen, fabric, even wood! Fibers can be dyed or left their natural color.

You can make:

Flower Baskets	Handbags	Trivets
Belts	Sewing Baskets	Picnic Baskets
Wastebaskets	Picture Frames	Baking Dish "Cozies"
Bread Baskets	Tote Bags	Hampers
Napkin Rings	Fruit Bowls	Placemats
Plant Holders	Rugs	Doormats

Note: Anyone can buy baskets cheaply at a discount store. Don't let this discourage you. Craft show customers are looking for handmade quality, not mass-produced products. Look for unique designs and embellishments. Use unique colors. Consider making basketweave handbags and other accessories.

Candle Making

Candles are useful as well as decorative items. They can be scented, unscented, dripless, round, square or free-form.

You can make animals, whimsical figures, centerpieces or historic "busts."

Clay

Clay is a great medium for whimsical figures as well as useful items. If you use natural clay, you will need a kiln, a special oven to set and dry your masterpieces. You don't necessarily have to buy one—your local ceramics store or workshop may allow you to use theirs for a per-piece or timeshare charge. Also, many synthetic clay compounds on the market don't require a kiln for drying and hardening. Check with your local craft supplier.

Ceramics are poured into molds while pottery is thrown and shaped on a pottery wheel. Both are fired to a hard finish in the kiln and then painted and/or glazed.

You can make:

Ornaments	Vases	Flowerpots
Magnets	Soup Tureens	Jewelry
Figurines	Mugs	Plates
Coasters	Candlesticks	Planters

Cookie Jars	Ashtrays	Baskets
Condiment Dishes	Clocks	

You could design your own coordinating sets—salt and pepper shakers, cream and sugar bowls, serving platters, or other combinations of tableware.

Cast Plaster

Less complicated and less costly than ceramics, cast plaster doesn't require any baking. The plaster compound is mixed with water and poured into premade molds. When dry, the product is sanded and painted or decorated.

You may have to experiment with different compounds to find the best mixture for your particular product—plaster can be brittle and may break easily. It may also be fragile to transport. If you have painting skills, this could be a wonderful medium for you. If you are looking for an economical craft, cast plaster is ideal.

You can make:

Christmas Tree Ornaments	Picture Frames	Wall Plaques
Clocks	Figurines	Magnets

Dough Art

Dough art can be lots of fun and the materials are ones you already have on hand. Pick one recipe or try all of them to see which one you like the best! *Creative clay* is made from cornstarch, baking soda and water. *Bread dough* is made from white bread (without the crust), white glue and glycerine. *Baker's clay* is made from salt, flour and water. (Exact ingredient proportions can be found in books on the subject.) Some dough needs to be baked and some just dries on its own. Dough can be painted or glazed, or you can color it by adding dye. Lots of flexibility!

You can make:

Whimsical Figures	Kitchen Magnets	Flowers
Jewelry	Baskets	Fruit
Miniatures	Ornaments	

Bread Dough Roses

Dough art is a relatively inexpensive craft with wonderful creative possibilities. Pictured here are roses made from a bread dough recipe.

Decoupage

This is the art of decorating an item with paper cutouts. The technique can be used on almost any surface. The picture is glued and then a varnish or a sealant is applied.

You could use:

Fairy-tale cutouts on baby nursery items

Floral pictures on lamps and picture frames

Herbs or flowers on garden accessories

Antique cutouts on Christmas ornaments

Victorian pictures on hatboxes

Tole and Folk Painting

Tole, decorative painting on metal, is a popular technique. This "primitive" art form is often used on antiques to make charming decorative items.

You could paint old tin watering cans, saw blades, antique furniture, wall plaques, canisters, tin mugs and coal buckets.

I've seen tole turn a tuna can into a work of art!

Glass

Glass is a medium that not too many new crafters consider. Although some glass crafts, such as glassblowing, are difficult and require extensive training and practice, others can be mastered in a reasonable amount of time.

Stained Glass

Pieces of colored and clear glass, arranged in a pattern, are joined with a soldering iron and lead.

Many wonderful things can be made from stained glass:

Jewelry	Wall Hangers	Mirror and Picture Frames
Jewelry Boxes	Cabinet Doors	Candleholders
Windows	Ornaments	Desk Accessories
Sun Catchers	Lamp Shades	

Or, you could make seasonal wall decorations such as teddy bears, Christmas wreaths, Easter bunnies or Christmas scenes.

Etched Glass

Think of all of the glass pieces you use every day—bowls, drinking glasses, glass jars and pitchers. Wouldn't they look nice with a little embellishment? A label or monogram?

Glass etching should be approached with care. Acid is applied to selected areas of clean glass to produce a design. The acid eats away at the glass and produces a "frosted" look when it is removed. Adequate ventilation is a must.

Consider etching:

Large glass bowls with fruit designs

Monogrammed wine glasses

Any kind of small empty jar with spice labels: oregano, thyme, etc.

Personalized ashtrays

Bathroom windows

Jewelry

Jewelry is a good craft choice if you don't have much space for your craft and its storage. But beware. There is an abundance of jewelry crafters out there, so if you plan to make jewelry your craft, make something unique! Be a little outrageous—or very old-fashioned!

Make one or a combination of:

Ankle Bracelets	Necklaces	Wrist Bracelets
Shoe Clips	Medallions	Earrings
Hat Pins	Tie Clips	Broaches

From:

Sterling Silver	Nickel	Brass
Silver Plate	Leather	Copper
Gold (10K, 14K, Gold-filled, etc.)		

With:

Enamel	Brass Beads	Ceramic
Old Watch Parts	Semiprecious Beads	Cut Stones (Lapidary)
Plastic Beads	Antique "Findings"	Crystals
Paper	Wood	Pearls
Indian Seed Beads	Clay	Dough
Paper Beads	Metal Beads	

Check your local "rock" supply to mine, cut and polish your own stones. You may be surprised at the variety of stones native to your own area and state.

Your first choice may be jewelry made from sterling silver and semiprecious stone beads, but this one is seriously overworked. Why not use pearls or synthetic diamonds with a metal other than silver?

If you still are set on the sterling and semiprecious combination, don't use standard settings. Have you ever heard of "wire-wrap" jewelry? Metal wires are woven into unique settings for stones or woven alone into bracelets and rings.

Or combine your jewelry making with another craft. Why not try origami earrings, macramé bracelets, stained glass earrings or ceramic broaches?

Bill, a jewelry crafter, made earrings of folded paper coated with a clear polyurethane. These were inexpensive and original. The material costs were minimal, and the profit margin was high.

Macramé

This craft uses cord tied in knot patterns to make decorative and useful household items. The supplies are not expensive and basic techniques are easy to learn. You can make plant hangers, wall decorations, key chains, necklaces, belts, bracelets and tote bags.

VERA SMITH AND HER "GEM TREES"

Who says that gemstones are only for jewelry? Vera Smith would disagree. She makes twisted wire trees with gemstone "flowers" and exhibits them mostly at gem and mineral shows.

Metals

Hard metals are often overlooked by new crafters, but they have some great possibilities. Metals such as iron can be made into items that are decorative as well as functional— and functional is definitely a plus in today's crafts market!

You could make:

Trivets	Fireplace Irons	Plant Holders
Gates and Railings	Weather Vanes	Signs
Candleholders	Sconces	Iron Sculptures

Softer, thinner metals can also be made into interesting products. They are easy to work with and require simple tools.

Tin Works

An ordinary tin can can be made into some very interesting and saleable products. Tin cans can be "punched" with different hole shapes and sizes to create intricate patterns or designs. The tin can also be curled, cut or folded. This is a wonderful medium for decorative candleholders because the candle light shines through the holes in the tin and creates a very nice effect.

The finished product can be either painted or varnished to preserve it and keep it from rusting. Other products can be applied to the tin to make it look aged or "antiqued."

If you're into recycling, what better way to use those tin cans that you and your friends normally throw away?

Copper Crafts

Working with copper is an ancient craft. The effects can vary from a shiny copper finish to a "verdigris" or oxidized look. Working with thin copper sheets or wire requires a minimum of tools.

You could use thin copper sheeting to make etched wall plaques of vintage cars, trains, abstract designs or historic scenes.

Copper jewelry can also be an effective and popular product line.

Leather

Leatherwork involves special tools, and animal hides are expensive, but this is a good craft if you plan to participate in craft shows. Since there aren't many leather crafters out there, your chances of being accepted at a craft show will be better.

Leather comes in many different weights, thicknesses and textures that will dictate somewhat the type of products you can make.

Cowhide is not your only choice. You might also want to consider doeskin, goatskin, chamois or suede. Practice and experiment on similar weight, less expensive materials before you try to cut and sew your expensive leather.

You can make:

Gloves	Hats	Jackets
Vests	Book Jackets	Eyeglass Cases
Change purses	Checkbook Covers	Jewelry
Wallets	Pouches	Bracelets
Buckles	Key Chain Charms	Belts
Handbags	Tote Bags	Bookmarks
Attaché Cases	Covered Bookends	Pen Holders
Letter Openers	Blotters	Ashtrays
Paperweights	Horse Tack (reins, bridles and saddles)	

Painting, Drawing and Photography

Though these may be shown and sold successfully at craft shows, they often sell better at art exhibits. If you like to draw, paint or take pictures, and you want to sell at craft shows, consider incorporating your artwork into more functional and smaller items.

Pen and ink notecards

Small whimsical sculptured characters

On-the-spot charcoal or ink portraits

Photographic postcards

Painting on wood, fabric, etc.

Watercolor greeting card sets

Small framed artwork

Calligraphy calendars, notecards, stationery, greeting cards, posters, etc.

If producing large paintings is what you like to do most, consider turning them into affordable art for the masses. Reproduce your artwork in limited edition poster form. Art posters can be popular products. Sell them framed or unframed.

Suppliers

Basketry: Connecticut Cane & Reed Company, Granite Lake Basketry

Cast Plaster: Bondex International

Candle Making: Barker Enterprises

Clay: Evenheat Kilns, Holland Molds, Lou Davis Wholesale

Clothing and Accessory Blanks: Bagworks, Dharma Trading Company, Qualin International

Fabrics and Fabric Accessories: American Handicrafts, The Astrup Company, Baer Fabrics, Carolina Mills, Clotilde, Inc., Coats & Clark, Dan River Company, Dazian Company, The Fabric Center, Fairfield Processing, Herrschners, Home Fabric Mills, Mary Maxim, Newark Dressmaker Supply, St. Louis Trimming Company, Susan Bates, Inc., Wm. E. Wright Company

Floral: Craven Pottery, Dried Materials Unlimited, Meadow Everlasting, San Francisco Herb Company, St. Louis Trimming Company, Wang's International

Glass: A.G.S.A. Glass Supplies, Delphi Stained Glass, Eastern Craft Supply

Jewelry: Greigers, T.B. Hagstroz & Son, Westcroft Beadworks

Leather: Fiebing Company, M. Siegel Company, Tandy Leather Company

Multiple Crafts: Dick Blick Art Materials

Paper Crafts: Lake City Crafts, Quill-It

Wood: Accents, Albert Constantine & Son, Leichtung Workshops, Midwest Dowel Works, Treasures, Woodworks

A.G.S.A. GLASS SUPPLIES
P.O. Box 2188
Zanesville OH 43702
Glass supplies

ACCENTS
P.O. Box 7387
Gonic NH 03839
Woodcraft patterns

ALBERT CONSTANTINE & SON
2050 Eastchester Rd.
Bronx NY 10461
Tools, plans, veneers, stains, kits

AMERICAN HANDICRAFTS
P.O. Box 2934
Ft. Worth TX 76113
Needlecraft and embroidery supplies

THE ASTRUP COMPANY
2937 W. 25th St.
Cleveland OH 44113
Canvas and awning fabrics

BAER FABRICS
515 E. Market St.
Louisville KY 40202
"Ultrasuede," linen, cotton

BAGWORKS
3933 California Pkwy. E.
Ft. Worth TX 76119
Canvas blanks—bags, aprons, etc.

BARKER ENTERPRISES
15106 10th Ave. SW
Seattle WA 98166
Candle-making supplies

BONDEX INTERNATIONAL
3616 Scarlet Oak Blvd.
St. Louis MO 63122
Plaster compound

CAROLINA MILLS
Box "V" Highway 76W
Branson MO 65616
Wool, blends, doubleknits

CLOTILDE INC.
2 Sew Smart Way
Stevens Point WI 54481
Sewing and quilting gadgets

COATS & CLARK
P.O. Box 1049
Laurinburg NC 28352
Threads, embroidery floss

CONNECTICUT CANE & REED COMPANY
134 Pine St.
Manchester CT 06040
Basket-making supplies

CRAVEN POTTERY
Pottery Rd.
Commerce GA 30529
Clay pots, florals, baskets

DAN RIVER COMPANY
Danville VA
(804) 799-7000
VIP fabrics

DAZIAN COMPANY
2014 Commerce St.
Dallas TX 75208
Satin, silk, taffeta, lamé

DELPHI STAINED GLASS
2116 E. Michigan Ave.
Lansing MI 48912
Stained glass kits, supplies, paints

DHARMA TRADING COMPANY
P.O. Box 150916
San Rafael CA 94915
A wide variety of cotton and silk blanks, wearable art supplies, fabric dyes, etc.

DICK BLICK ART MATERIALS
(800) 447-8192 (call for catalog)

DICK BLICK WEST
P.O. Box 521
Henderson NV 89015

DICK BLICK CENTRAL
P.O. Box 1267
Galesburg IL 61401

DICK BLICK EAST
P.O. Box 26
Allentown PA 18105
Easels, paints, brushes, palettes, paint organizers, print-making and drawing papers, tracing and layout papers, silhouette papers and instructions, origami papers, construction paper, precut mat frames, matboard and mat cutters, picture frames, all kinds of markers and chalks, pencils, pens, inks, air-brushes, screen printing supplies, clay supplies and modeling and sculpting materials, instruction videos and books for quilling, origami, silhouette art and other paper crafts, macramé twine and cord, knotting boards, rings and hangers, metal punch tools for tin work and copper crafts, copper, aluminum and brass foil sheets, copper tooling molds and metal punch designs

DRIED MATERIALS UNLIMITED
1584 Highland Ave., Rte 10
Cheshire CT 06410
Dried baby's breath, eucalyptus, etc.

EASTERN CRAFT SUPPLY
P.O. Box 341
Wyckoff NJ 07481
Glass etching and engraving supplies

EVENHEAT KILNS
6949 Legion Rd.
Caseville MI 48725
Kilns and supplies

THE FABRIC CENTER
P.O. Box 8212
Fitchburg MA 01420-8212
Coordinated home decorating fabrics

FAIRFIELD PROCESSING
P.O. Box 1130
Danbury CT 06813
Batting, fiberfill, etc.

FIEBING COMPANY
516 S. Second St.
Milwaukee WI 53204
Leather dyes and finishes

GRANITE LAKE BASKETRY
Star Rt. Box 16
Mohawk MI 49950
Basketry supplies

GREIGERS
P.O. Box 93070
Pasadena CA 91109
Gemstones, beads, lapidary equipment and supplies

HERRSCHNERS
Hoover Rd.
Stevens Point WI 54481
Needlecraft kits and supplies

HOLLAND MOLDS
P.O. Box 5021
Trenton NJ 08638
Ceramic molds, etc.

HOME FABRIC MILLS
882 S. Main St.
Cheshire CT 06410
Chintz and prints

LAKE CITY CRAFTS
Rt. 1, Box 637
Highlandeville MO 65669
Quilling paper, tools and kits

LEICHTUNG WORKSHOPS
4944 Commerce Parkway
Cleveland OH 44128
Hand and power tools for wood crafters

LOU DAVIS WHOLESALE
1490 Elkhorn Rd.
Lake Geneva WI 53147
Ceramic and doll supplies

M. SIEGEL COMPANY
120 Pond St.
Ashland MA 01721
Leather hides, accessories, tools

MARY MAXIM
2001 Holland Ave.
Port Huron MI 48061-5019
Yarns, floss, thread, needlecraft supplies

MEADOW EVERLASTING
16464 Shabbona Rd.
Malta IL 60150
Rosebuds, statice, etc.

MIDWEST DOWEL WORKS
4631 Hutchinson Rd.
Cincinnati OH 45248
Dowels, pegs, etc.

NEWARK DRESSMAKER SUPPLY
P.O. Box 2448
Lehigh Valley PA 18001
Dressmaker and needlecraft supplies

QUALIN INTERNATIONAL
P.O. Box 31145
San Francisco CA 94131
Natural white silk blanks—scarves, ties, garments, fabric

QUILL-IT
P.O. Box 130
Elmhurst IL 60126
Quilling supplies and paper

SAN FRANCISCO HERB COMPANY
250 14th St.
San Francisco CA 94103
Dried herbs

ST. LOUIS TRIMMING COMPANY
5040 Arsenal St.
St. Louis MO 63139
Ribbon, gimp, rattail, trim, also floral wire, tape, bridal
   accessories

SUSAN BATES, INC.
8 Shelter Dr.
Greer SC 29650
Sewing notions, knitting and crochet tools

T.B. HAGSTROZ & SON
709 Sansom St.
Philadelphia PA 19106
Jewelry-making tools, supplies, equipment

TANDY LEATHER COMPANY
P.O. Box 2934
Ft. Worth TX 46113
Leather kits, tools, instructions

TREASURES
P.O. Box 9
Huntsville OH 43324
Plans and patterns for furniture and household pieces

WANG'S INTERNATIONAL
4250 Shelby Dr.
Memphis TN 38181
Silk, berries, ribbon, etc.

WESTCROFT BEADWORKS
139 Washington Dr.
South Norwalk CT 06854
Beads, beads and more beads!

WM. E. WRIGHT COMPANY
South Street
West Warren MA 01092
Lace, ruffles, ribbon, trim

WOODWORKS
4500 Anderson Blvd.
Ft. Worth TX 76117
Unfinished wood pieces

CHAPTER WORKSHEET

This worksheet will help you select the right craft from the many exciting choices available. Even if you already have a favorite craft, this worksheet will give you ideas for new crafts to try or new directions to pursue.

My hobbies, interests and talents:

_____   _____

_____   _____

_____   _____

Crafts and craft products I have tried or made in the past.

_____	Loved!	Liked	Just OK	Disliked
_____	Loved!	Liked	Just OK	Disliked
_____	Loved!	Liked	Just OK	Disliked
_____	Loved!	Liked	Just OK	Disliked

Crafts equipment I already have and like to use (knitting needles, sewing machine, scroll saw, paints, etc.):

_____   _____

_____   _____

Possible themes or special interests I could incorporate into my crafts:

_____   _____

_____   _____

_____   _____

Crafts or mediums I have always wanted to work with or have some talent or experience with:

Wood:	cutting	carving	other _____
Florals and naturals:	arranging	pressing	growing	herbs
	other _____			
Fabric:	sewing	patchwork	quilting	appliqué
	other _____			
Yarn or thread:	weaving	crochet	knitting	embroidery	needlepoint
	crewel	tatting	cross-stitch	smocking	other ____
Paper:	quilling	papier-mâché		silhouette art
	origami	other _____		
Clay:	ceramics	pottery	other _____

Glass:	stained glass		glass etching		
	other _____				
Jewelry:	sterling	silver plate	14k gold	10k gold	
	gold-filled	copper	nickel	brass	leather
	other _____				

	with:	enamel	plastic beads
		paper	clay
		simulated diamonds	semiprecious beads
		brass beads	antique "findings"
		wood	dough
		pearls	precious stones
		ceramic	crystals
		Indian seed beads	metal beads
		other _____	

Metals:	pewter	iron	copper	tin
	other _____			
Leather:	hard	soft	other _____	
Art:	pastels	charcoal	pen and ink	acrylics	photography
	sculpture	calligraphy	watercolors	other _____	
Other:	basketry	cast plaster	candlemaking	
	decoupage	macramé	dough art	

CHAPTER THREE

DEFINING YOUR PRODUCT LINE

Choosing a craft and defining your product line go hand in hand. While you are exploring your many craft options, you should also be looking ahead to your product line—all the products and "sub-products" that you will make.

When considering a particular medium or craft, consider its expansion possibilities as well as its limitations. This foresight will help you avoid a dead end when you want to expand your line.

Write down the products you would make from a craft you are considering. Can you list only a few? Maybe those are all you will need—in different sizes and/or colors. Or maybe the craft is too limited for your visions and talents. Consider mixing more than one craft with a common theme. Are there so many that you can't write them down fast enough? Then be more specific. Narrow the field to a manageable level by targeting a particular consumer group, such as children, or a particular theme, such as gardens.

Your product line should:
- Have focus and continuity with one dominant theme
- Be easily explained with one concise descriptive phrase
- Consist of complete products that need no additional items to make them useable
- Have products that enable you to use all your leftover scraps
- Consist of large, medium and small products
- Consist of products that vary in price

It is always best to start with a simple and concise product line that can be easily defined and managed. Later, as your creativity and craft expertise increase, you can add new products to it. Start small and plan carefully.

One of the greatest mistakes that new crafters make is to branch out in many directions without focus. An initial plan of your prospective product line will motivate you. While you are working on one product, you can look forward to the next one.

In essence, you should specialize. Having "a little of this" and "a little of that" with no particular rhyme or reason will confuse you *and* your customers, and it will not make you the quality crafter who will be successful in this competitive marketplace.

You can test the focus of your product line by trying to explain it in one concise descriptive phrase. When you submit an application to participate in a craft show, the show promoters want to know what products you will be displaying. They do not want a disjointed list of items: "some florals, some wood, picture frames and jewelry." They want a concise descriptive phrase that gives them this information: "children's wooden toys" or "fabric kitchen accessories" or "handmade baskets" or "pottery tableware." This is a description of your *product line.* You might expand it slightly to "pottery tableware—plates, mugs, bowls, etc.," but there won't be room for much more.

This is not to say that you shouldn't have a variety of products. You should. But select them carefully. Always have high-priced items, medium-priced items and low-priced items. Also, a variety of large, medium and small products can keep you competitive in any selling environment. By making products that appeal to a variety of customers, you will be assured that you have products that each customer can afford.

Keep this "large, medium, small" approach in mind while you are considering the many product options within a particular craft or medium. Let's say you are going to make wooden products. Don't produce all large pieces. First, they will be hard to transport. Second, not all people can afford them. Even the person who can afford a large, pricey wood bookcase may not have the transportation to carry it home. But that customer may be very interested in a book*shelf*—a smaller, less expensive item with the same basic function and design.

Having a product line of graduated sizes can also allow you to make the most of leftover scraps and raw materials. This will minimize waste and maximize profits.

If your medium if fabric, for example, you could make tablecloths, table runners, napkins and placemats, hot pads and napkin rings. If your medium is leather, you could make large totebags, handbags, wallets, belts, belt buckles and key chains.

Applying this frugal thinking will reduce the space you need for your crafts, too, since you will have virtually no scraps left over from your work. All of your raw material will be used productively, *and* your product line will have a theme, *and* you will have focus, *and* it will greatly improve your profits!

Finally, your products should be complete. Selling a pendant without a chain or a picture without a frame—or at least matting—is self-defeating.

Ways to Define Your Line

Your product line can be dictated and defined by any one or more of the following.
- Medium—what your product is made from
- Craft—how the medium is worked
- Product—what you make from the medium
- Shape
- Consumer—who will actually use it
- Season—when it will be used
- Location—where it will be used
- Era—when it was used originally
- Finish—how your product is decorated or treated
- Size
- Special interest and mixed media

Defining by Medium

The first question you will ask yourself is "What will my products be made of?" Will you make only wood items? Will you only work with flowers? or clay? or fabric? It is best to select only one medium and to explore it fully.

Don't assume that anything that can be made from that medium has already been made. New craft ideas pop up constantly. Be the first with a new idea and you have a decided advantage. Don't worry about others copying it. Someone will always try. If your idea is really unusual, you may want to *patent* or *copyright* it. You may even approach a crafts publisher about writing a how-to book on your product. On the other hand, just because you thought of it *first* doesn't mean you thought of it *best*. Others may take your idea and add ideas of their own. So you should be thinking of new ways to use it, ways to make it better or new markets for it.

Below, I have taken some of the mediums listed in chapter two and grouped related products to create a common *theme*. This should be your goal. You may want to group the items differently or add other items. That's OK. These examples are provided to stimulate your imagination and show you focused product lines.

You may want to start by making only one product. Then, as you progress, you could add some of the other products listed on the same line or in the same category. Ultimately, you may want the whole *category* as your product line. But it is better to start small until you have a clearer picture of what the customer wants.

As you start selling, your customers will show you by their purchases and comments which products you should keep and which you should delete from your product line.

Wood

This is a medium with lots of options. Start with a manageable (but related) product line. You can always expand later, when you know better what will sell.

TOYS

- trains, boats, airplanes, cars—You could make wooden trains your only product and make them life-size (large enough for a child to sit in), play size (small enough for a child to handle), or miniature (as a collectible). You could specialize in trains and trains only—and make them in all three sizes!
- puzzles, games—Your product line could be of only children's games and puzzles, or you could cater to the child in every adult and make interesting "brain teasers."
- marionettes, puppets, jumping jacks—All children have a fascination for marionettes and puppets: animals, clowns, storybook heroes and heroines, mythical creatures, etc. Not too many crafters make them.
- dolls, doll furniture—Dolls and doll furniture are popular not only with children but also with many adult doll collectors.
- toy chests, wagons, desks, stools, chairs—Parents, grandparents, aunts and uncles love to shop for the little ones in their lives.

FURNITURE AND ACCESSORIES

- outdoor tables, chairs, tea carts, barbeque stands, picnic benches, snack trays, etc.—A popular spring product line.
- cutting boards, trivets, coasters, trays, towel racks, tea cart, jelly cabinet—Functional items used in almost every household.
- plaques, clocks, frames—Wonderful decorating accents. Clocks are always popular.
- shelves, night stands, headboards, armoires, lingerie chests, etc.—Develop your own decorative line of furniture!

- coffee/end tables, card tables, bookcases, bookends, shelves—Serviceable items are always good sellers.
- CD holders, videotape organizers, audio tape caddies—Everyone uses them!

JEWELRY

- bracelets and earrings
- wood bead necklaces and ornately carved broaches
- belt buckles
- jewelry boxes (men's and women's)

Women and men alike love to "spoil" themselves with these trinkets and accessories.

Try to focus on one particular theme within your medium. Here are two categories, each with some "sub-themes" that could be used for product lines.

GARDEN

- birdhouses—A charming product line!
- garden markers, planters—Sure to be a springtime success!
- whirligigs, weather vanes—Homeowners love these!

CARVED FIGURES

- whimsical characters—For the child in all of us.
- animals and birds—From decoys to planters to decorative accents, you'll never get bored.
- well-known characters—Santa Claus, Uncle Sam—Collectibles for the discriminating buyer.

Fabric

Fabric is another medium with so many choices that it is easy to lose focus.

HOUSEHOLD

- napkins, tablecloths, table runners, napkin rings, placemats—Especially for the holidays!
- towels, shower curtains, fabric-covered mirrors, coordinated accessories—Let your imagination run wild.
- quilts, comforters, decorated pillowcases, fabric picture frames, mirrors, wastebaskets, lamp shades, wall fans, throw rugs—Coordinate a whole room. Sell the pieces in sets or individually.

- chair pads, stool covers, folding chair covers, slip covers—These items always need replacing.
- appliance covers, pot holders, hot plates, oven mitts, aprons—Coordinate and decorate in charming country prints, bold stripes, comfortable plaids, homey gingham or go-with-anything solids.

FOR CHILDREN
- doll clothing with matching children's dresses—A charming idea!
- dollhouse accessories: rugs, quilts, pillows, bed linens, tablecloths, etc.—Popular accessories for collectors.
- aprons: for cooking, for painting, for "helping mom," etc.—You could really have fun with this one!

PERSONAL
- handbags, totebags, duffle bags—Do women ever have enough of these?
- ring cases, jewelry travelers, shoe caddies, covered clothes hangers—Serviceable and decorative all in one.
- travel shoe bags, ties and hankies, garment bags, shaving bags, etc.—Why shouldn't we pamper the menfolk too?

Defining by Craft

You may want to use one medium *and* limit the type of *craft* within that medium. For example, if your medium is fabric, your craft could be limited to quilted items such as baby quilts, or quilted vests. Is your medium paper? Try to specialize in one craft type, such as quilling *or* origami.

You can't do everything and do it well. Explore one craft to the fullest. Find new products to make from it. Find new ways to improve upon old ideas. Be original. Be creative. Your focus on one craft will bring you very positive results. Also, remember that different crafts require different tools. If you are considering more than one craft, you may need different tools for each craft. That can get expensive.

Defining by Product

You may want to use only one medium (what your product is made of), select a specific craft (how you "work" that medium), and define your product line still further by the product itself.

JIM FOWLER—A MASTER OF HIS CRAFT

Jim Fowler was a welder by trade. But after he moved from New Hampshire to Richmond, Virginia, the economy left him jobless. Unemployed but resourceful and creative, Jim looked to himself for an answer. And he found it. After seeing a piece of wire-wrapped jewelry in a local store, Jim bought a book on the subject and taught himself the art of wire-wrapping.

Wire-wrapping involves forming precious metal wires (gold, silver, etc.) into intricate jewelrydesigns. Plain gold rings can be made by intertwining the wires into a basketweave pattern, for example. Intricately woven strands of gold or silver can also be made into a ring or pendant with a prong setting that will hold faceted stones. For beginners, simple braided bracelets can be made from the same basic technique.

Jim Fowler started his business and made his first jewelrypieces at the dining room table of the apartment that he shared with his wife, Selina. He had a love of fine things and combined his wire-wrap jewelry with large high-quality semiprecious stones. His designs are original. His technique is craftsmanship at its finest. It's no wonder Jim Fowler draws a crowd at any craft or gem and jewelry show he attends.

Let's take clay as an example. Clay is your medium. You are going to use ceramic molds (defining further by craft) and make flowerpots and flowerpots *only* (defining further still by product). The possibilities are still endless and you have narrowed your choices down by defining in three ways: by medium (clay), then by craft (ceramics), and finally by product (flowerpots).

Initially, this may sound boring. But think of all the different size flowerpots you can make! Think of unusual shapes—square, round, oval. Think of how you will decorate them! You might want to decorate them in only a few of your own "trademark" patterns or you may want to make each design unique. You could make and sell them in sets of graduated sizes or sell them individually—or both! You may want to design only *herb* pots—all the same size and all the same shape. Yes, the possibilities are still extensive and yet you have focused on a *manageable* product line.

Suppose your medium is wood and your craft is hand carving. You might want to limit yourself initially to *hand-carved* (craft) *wood* (medium) *clocks* (product).

Again, the possibilities are still endless! There are many different types of wood. There are many different wood finishes, paints and stains to choose from. You could also vary the sizes and functions—hand-carved wood *wall* clocks, hand-carved wood *grandfather* clocks, small hand-carved wood *table* clocks!

If you are especially talented and become easily bored, you might want to limit yourself to one product and eventually vary and explore different mediums and crafts. Clocks can be made out of clay, wood, plaster, and many other mediums.

This is one of the criteria that I used to produce my own original product line. My product line description reads: "Christmas tree skirts—in all sizes, colors and fabrics."

Defining by Shape

Do you want to stop here—defining only by medium, craft and product? If you still find yourself with too many options, you might want to further define by shape.

The *clay* (medium) *pottery* (craft) *flowerpots* (product) could all have the same unusual shape. Get the picture?

For the product line of clocks, you could make *square* (shape) *carved* (craft) *wood* (medium) *clocks* (product).

Defining by Consumer

You might want to target a specific consumer, the person who will use the product.

Children's items are popular and always seem to sell well. Men's items are often overlooked. Men don't usually go to craft shows but the women in their lives do. Men's products are often hard to find at a craft show. Consider such items as apparel and accessories or desk sets. It could make your booth very popular (and successful) at a craft show.

You could make *men's* (consumer) *silk* (medium) *hand-painted* (craft) *ties and pocket hankies* (product). You could expand later to include women's ties or other men's silk or fabric accessories. But ties and hankies would be a good start.

Defining by Season

There is much that you can do within this genre and, contrary to public belief, a well-thought-out seasonal item will sell most of the year—especially if it is a "collectible" such as an original Santa Claus figurine or a decorated egg.

People no longer shop for Christmas just at Christmastime. They shop most of the year for both decorative items and gifts and generally buy them when they see them.

Hand-carved, hand-decorated eggs are also a popular collector's item. In fact, they don't sell especially well at Easter time, but they do sell throughout the year. Pysanky eggs (Ukranian egg art), real eggs with cutout lace designs (done with a high-speed drill), eggs with scenes inside, burned wood eggs, decoupage eggs, eggs dressed up to look like a figure or person, the traditional painted egg, the gilt egg, ostrich eggs, goose eggs, etc.—there are so many.

Actually, you could do seasonal items throughout the year and never get bored. Think of all the different holidays and the different colors associated with each season— people love to decorate for each holiday!

Valentine's Day (red)

St. Patrick's Day (green)

Spring/Easter (pastels)

4th of July (red, white and blue)

Halloween (orange and black)

Autumn/Thanksgiving (rusts, orange, brown, gold)

Christmas (red, green, plaid, metallic)

You could literally develop one product and tailor it to the different holidays and seasons. For example, door decorations or fabric flags or mailbox covers herald the coming of any one of the above events.

Knitted and crocheted items can also make up a seasonal product line—light

"Lace" Egg

This intricately carved egg would be a wonderful addition to any egg collection. The lovely pattern was carved c-a-r-e-f-u-l-l-y with a high-speed drill. The artist thoughtfully completed the product package by encasing her design in a glass dome display.

cotton nautical sweaters, vests and cardigans for summer and heavier sweaters, mittens, hats and slippers for the colder seasons.

Don't sell for just the current season. Have samplings of all your seasonal products, with the most stock being for the current season. If your customers like your products for autumn, they might purchase their winter apparel or decorations at the same time.

Defining by Location

After you have defined your product line by medium, craft, and any other criteria that you have selected, you may decide to further define it by location—*where* it will be used.

For example, you might further define our hand-carved wood clock by its location: *square* (shape) *carved* (craft) *wood* (medium) ***mantle*** (location) *clocks* (product).

This may seem creatively confining to you at first, but you will be surprised at the many different designs you will think of once you put your mind to it.

Location could be your main criterion: coordinated kitchen items, bath accessories, outdoor lawn furniture, children's room furnishings, or closet accessories.

Defining by Era

Different periods in history have produced different patterns of workmanship and design. You could further define your product line by focusing on a particular era: *Victorian* floral arrangements, *Early American* furniture and accessories, *contemporary* wall hangings, *1940s* jewelry.

Or, to use the clock example again, you could make it a *square* (shape) **Victorian** (era) *carved* (craft) *wood* (medium) *mantle* (location) *clock* (product). You see?

Defining by Finish

How you *decorate* or *treat* your products may be the sole reason that your products stand out from the crowd. You could use the same decoration throughout your product line to tie it all together.

Tole painting can be applied to many different mediums: tin cans, wood plaques, iron coal buckets, etc. Decoupage can be applied to many different items to give them a unique look. You could keep the same paper cutout patterns or designs and decorate coordinated items that complement each other. All of your items could be decorated with sunflowers or roses or pineapples or clowns!

Defining by Size

You may choose to work only with large pieces. Perhaps your designs are too intricate to apply to smaller items.

Or maybe your work space is limited and you are overwhelmed by the thought of working on and completing large projects and products. Well then, you may decide to produce your product line in miniature. Almost every product listed in these chapters can be made in miniature. They can also be made life-sized or bigger than life!

Special Interest and Mixed Media

Special interest product lines can be very popular and offer you more *craft* variety and the opportunity to incorporate different *mediums* into one product line. For example:

KATHRYN
CARLUCCI—TOLE
PAINTING

Kathryn Carlucci studied commercial and fine art at Paier School of Art in Hamden, Connecticut. When she moved to Newtown, Connecticut, in 1971, she studied tole painting from a well-known local artist. And Kathryn's tole paintings are a work of art. She paints local landmarks, buildings and eighteenth-century designs on breadboxes, bowls, canisters, old coffee pots, wall plaques, milk cans—almost anything. But Kathryn is most noted for her wonderful paintings of the town where she lives. Her Main Street scenes are by far her most popular.

She originally started painting as a hobby, but it soon turned into a small business. Now Kathryn's dream is to open her own shop selling her tole painted creations.

Gardening	*Sports*
Clay flowerpots	Plaster team clocks
Fabric aprons and knee pads	Wood sports plaques
Wood garden markers	Fabric jerseys
Decorated metal tools	Ceramic sports figures

Mixed media, if done right, makes for an interesting yet focused display and product line. You can combine any crafts and mediums. For example, your product line could contain wax candles and ceramic candlesticks; or fabric dolls and wood doll furniture. How about macramé plant hangers and painted pottery flowerpots! There are so many creative ways to combine different ideas into an interesting product line!

Mixed media and special interest are great product lines if your business will be the combined efforts of several crafters. You may have a friend who sews, another who makes ceramic pieces, while your specialty is wood. Individually, the three of you may not have the time to produce enough finished product to make a good showing at a craft show. Maybe the three of you enjoy your crafts but don't want to—or can't—devote enough time to create the substantial inventory needed to participate in craft shows. *Together,* using one theme, you and your friends can produce a very successful—and interesting—product line.

This can also be very economical both in time and money. Three of you will pay for only one booth space—split three ways. All three of you don't have to be present at every show. You could rotate shows and spend more time with your families while still running a successful crafts business.

Examples of Well-Defined Product Lines

Whatever craft (or crafts) you choose, your product line should always have a central theme—your products should be related somehow. You should be able to describe your product line in one phrase—not list your products, but *describe* your product line: "stained pine household furniture," "painted wood toys," "hand-carved Victorian wood mantle clocks."

If you cannot think of a concise description, your product line is probably too cluttered.

Here are some actual product lines from real crafters:

ANTHONY

Lace Eggs

Product: eggs only

Craft: cut with a high-speed drill

These are real chicken, goose and ostrich eggs decorated with openwork "lace" designs cut out with a high-speed drill. His products are complete—each egg is sold in a glass dome stand ready to display. The shapes are basically the same; the sizes and designs vary.

MIRIAH

Plaster Sextagonal Wall Clocks

Medium and Craft: cast plaster

Product: clocks

Size: they're all the same size

Shape: every one of them has six sides

What makes these products so popular and unique is their varied decorations. Each clock is decorated with different decorator fabric designs, popular children's motifs, country prints, hunt scenes—you name it! There is a clock to match any home decor and every room in that home.

LORETTA

Marbleized Silk Personal Accessories—scarves, earrings, neckties, hankies

Medium: silk fabric

Craft and Decoration: the marbleizing technique produces a swirl pattern on all of her accessories

The colors vary and there are a variety of different products to choose from.

LAURA

Decoupage Miniatures

Medium: wood

Craft: decoupage

Product: wall plaques

Size: miniature

These miniature wood wall plaques are decoupaged with different pictures. The shapes and pictures vary.

JIM

Painted Wood Children's Toys

Medium: wood

Craft: cut and design

Consumer: children

Decorations: all painted in primary colors

SARAH

Wall designs and home decorating accents made with pressed flowers

Medium: florals

Craft: she presses and arranges her flowers

Sarah arranges her pressed flowers into wall plaque scenes, glass-domed paperweights, as borders for picture frames, and much, much more!

MARILYN

Bread Dough Roses

Medium: bread dough

Craft: sculpting the roses

Product: roses only

All of Marilyn's roses are made from a bread dough recipe. They are wrapped in floral paper with ferns, just like real roses would be.

TERRANCE

Turned Wood Bowls

Medium: wood

Craft: turned on a lathe

Product: bowls

Shape: round only—no ovals

Terrance's product line consists of round wood bowls in a large variety of sizes.

Building Your Product Line

In your quest for the perfect product combinations, your product line may evolve through several stages. You may start with one type of product and find that it doesn't sell quite as well as expected. Don't be discouraged. As you discover what *does* sell, you will expand that part of your product line.

Product development is an ongoing process. You should always be adding new

CARLA
SCHARTNER—
MAKING NEW
FROM OLD

While many crafters choose to work with new materials, some crafters favor recycling old products into new products. Carla Schartner has built a marvelous product line fashioned from recycled windows. Carla calls her products "Mirrored Windows" because that's exactly what they are. They are old windows that are stripped, refinished and decorated. But instead of replacing the panes of broken window glass, Carla substitutes mirrors where the windows should be.

Everyone knows that mirrors appear to enlarge a room. Carla's mirrored windows do more than just enlarge—they enhance. Her designs range from sponge painted, stained, "crackle"

painted (to give an old effect) and stencilled to those decorated with flowers.

Carla had not intended to get into the crafts business. She had seen a mirrored window she liked in an antique store, but it was very expensive. So she made her own. Before long, her sisters asked her to make windows for their homes.

Once Carla's sisters' friends saw her designs, they wanted one too. So with no more training than refinishing a few pieces of furniture for her own home, Carla began making her products for other people. That's when she started asking friends if they thought other people would actually pay money for her products.

Her friends said *yes*, and

Carla's business in mirrored windows was founded. She knew by prior response that she had found a product that would sell. And she knew that she could produce them and decorate them for a reasonable price—much more reasonably than the antique stores were selling them for—and still make a reasonable profit. Carla had enough inventory to start selling her products at craft shows about a year after she made her first window.

Carla remembers her first few craft shows, "At first I charged too little for my products and I was afraid to sell myself." But eventually, she got her prices fixed and learned to "sell herself" and her products to the customers.

products and deleting old products as they start to show a decline in sales.

Here's how my own product line evolved.

I started making crafts about ten years ago. Christmas was my favorite holiday season. I don't know what led me to make my first Christmas tree skirt, but I enjoyed designing it, I liked the process of making it, and I *loved* the finished product and how it looked under a fully decorated Christmas tree.

My first tree skirt was completely hand sewn. It took a very long time to make. When I decided to try to sell my product, I realized that I didn't have time to make them all by hand. So I got a sewing machine.

Also, my original tree skirt was lovingly hand-appliquéd with many Christmas motifs and scenes. I could not make *all* of my products with such intricate patterns and produce a competitive product line.

I simplified the pattern and made a few simple red-white-and-green tree skirts, but I soon discovered that not everyone has red, white and green on their Christmas tree. When I looked at my friends' and family's trees, they were all different. Some used lots of metallic ornaments. Others had very old-fashioned trees with antique ornaments. Still others liked their Christmas tree, its ornaments and decorations to reflect a more formal lifestyle and complement their home's decor in pinks, peaches, blues and mauves. And finally, some had "country" homes with tiny country prints throughout.

So I added some country Christmas prints to my product line. These and the red-white-green skirts were all I had time to make for my first season of craft shows. They didn't sell particularly well. At some shows, they didn't sell at all. So I tried other fabrics—gold and silver lamé, and moire taffeta in muted shades.

It took me two Christmas seasons before I discovered *why* my products weren't selling. (I'm a slow learner.) This is what I learned:

(1) I wasn't displaying them so that people could *see* them. They were laid on a table, and most people didn't even know what they were!

(2) It wasn't the *fabric* choices that were at fault. It was the *size* of the tree skirts that made them not sell.

I was making them too small. Sure, they fit under my apartment-sized artificial tree, but most people bought very full real trees for which my tree skirts were just too small. And, customers who were interested in the same size items as I was selling could already buy them at most stores—cheaper than I could make them.

This brings us to a very important point. Don't try to compete with a product that is already on the market and is widely mass produced. You can't. Try to make your products unique so they can't be bought anyplace else but from you.

I found that anyone could purchase an average-sized tree skirt at almost any store very cheaply, *but* very large skirts were almost impossible to find. If your Christmas tree was taller than six feet, the mass-produced skirts were just too small. If you had cathedral ceilings and bought a fifteen-foot tree, there was just nowhere to buy a skirt for it.

The other thing I learned was many apartment dwellers and senior citizens used very small tabletop trees simply because they didn't have room for anything larger. So I used my leftover fabric and trim scraps to make tabletop tree skirts in all the same patterns and designs as my larger skirts. These sold well also.

I also enhanced my display so that all of my products were visible to the customer. A friend made some racks for me so my product could be displayed upright and could be seen better.

I also added some large and very large tree skirts to my product line. At my very next show, I knew I was on the right track. The larger skirts sold very well. Even the average-sized skirts sold better because now they could be seen. It was my first success as a crafter and I was hooked. I came home with a considerable amount of cash. That was all the encouragement I needed.

Each year I built my product line a little more by adding a new fabric, some new designs, some outrageous combinations and some really "glitzy" pieces. I can honestly say that now I have a tree skirt for every home somewhere in my display. And I have a tree skirt for every pocketbook, from expensive hand-appliquéd, patchwork and tapestry skirts to simple Christmas prints made from less-expensive fabrics.

I expanded my product line, but only after my tree skirt inventory and production was well within my control. I included ornaments to match the tree skirts to give each tree a "total look." I made original Santa and angel dolls, and miniature decorated Christmas trees both to match my tree skirts and to stand on their own. These smaller products helped my sales tremendously when I found myself selling in a less affluent community. Now, my product line has focus and variety and, most importantly, it works!

A successful product line takes time to build. The process can't be rushed. To a certain extent, it is by trial and error. You may make a few wrong turns and have to make adjustments along the way before you come up with a formula for success. Take your time and learn from your customers. They will be your most valuable source of information.

Trends and Timing

Every product has a life cycle. Only occasionally will you find a product that is truly "timeless."

Pay attention to what is going on around you. Read trend publications such as

The Popcorn Report by Faith Popcorn. Buy a copy of a men's magazine as well as women's publications. Browse through some decorating magazines and home improvement publications.

You may be able to capitalize on a current trend. The trick is to recognize when you are hitting the fad at the beginning, when it has already reached its peak, and when it is on the decline.

Recently I read a feature article in my local newspaper about a crafter I know very well. She was introducing a "new" product line and had gotten the newspaper to interview her for a story on her new line. I was very disappointed to read the article. The products that she was just "introducing" have already been on the market for quite some time. Many people already own them, and the product is now extensively mass produced and marketed. Her chances of being successful are limited.

CHAPTER WORKSHEET

A successful crafter needs a distinctive and focused range of related products to sell. This worksheet will help you define your product line so you can describe it in one concise phrase. After completing this worksheet, return here and complete the following:

My product line can be described in one concise descriptive phrase as follows:

_____

I have decided to define my product line by the following criteria:

Explain:

Medium (what the product is made from)   _____

_____

_____

Craft (how the medium is worked)   _____

_____

_____

Product (what is made from that medium)   _____

_____

_____

Shape (square, round, etc.)   _____

_____

_____

Consumer (who will use it)   _____

_____

_____

Season (when it will be used)   _____

_____

_____

Location (where it will be used)   _____

_____

_____

Era (when it was used)   _____

_____

_____

Decorations (how the product is finished)

_____

_____

_____

Size (miniature, life-sized, etc.)

_____

_____

_____

What actual products will I make?
Large Products:

_____

_____

_____

Medium Products:

_____

_____

_____

Small Products:

_____

_____

_____

If I decide to expand my product line, the next most likely choices might be:

Large:

_____

_____

_____

Medium:

_____

_____

_____

Small:

_____

_____

CHAPTER FOUR

THE BUSINESS OF CRAFTS

As much fun as it is to just make crafts, there are areas you need to address if you are going to turn your crafts into a profitable and organized *business*.

Now, don't be intimidated by the word "business." You may not consider yourself a businessperson, but the business end of your crafts is fairly easy to organize and control. It's simply a matter of plus and minus—and keeping track of both. To be successful you need to watch your expenditures and keep accurate records of your sales. If you do this, everything else will fall into place.

Every unnecessary dollar you spend—on raw materials, bank fees, licensing, taxes, advertising, etc.—will be that much less you have in your pocket. So you need to examine costs carefully to determine which expenses are necessary and which can be reduced.

But first, you need to explore the basic foundations of your business.

- Your inventory is very important. You need to keep track of how much you have, its value and where it is.
- You need to have adequate insurance coverage—health, damage and liability.
- You should have a separate bank account to monitor expenses, sales and profit.
- If you sell taxable products, you must apply for a sales tax number.
- To make the most of your selling opportunities, you should accept a variety of payment forms—cash, personal checks, and at least one major credit card.

DEBBIE BARTON— QUILTER AND ACCOUNTANT

Debbie Barton is luckier than most crafters when it comes to handling the business end of crafting. She's a self-employed Certified Public Accountant, so she already has the basic accounting knowledge and information that she needs to run a small business.

Debbie is also a quilter. She loves to create her own unique patterns on her computer and then make those designs come to life on an actual quilt.

Though Debbie is just starting to participate in craft shows,- she is definitely on the right track. She has armed herself with a professional-looking display (made by her husband) and a large variety of quilts. She also completes her quilt sets with matching pillow cases, a very practical and profitable idea.

In addition to the time-consuming, expensive, intricately patterned full-size quilts that Debbie sells, she has also added "pillow quilts" to her product line. These pillow quilts take less time to produce than full-size traditional quilts. And because they are not as labor intensive, they can be sold at a much lower price. This will make Debbie's product line and prices competitive in any selling environment.

Because she has had consistent success since she started selling from her home, Debbie has wisely taken the time to produce a large inventory of these pillow quilts. When she goes to a show, she is sure to have products that appeal to every taste and budget.

Inventory

Consider your inventory as "money in the bank." Pieces yet to be sold represent future cash. Anything in stock is part of your "savings account." Of course, your goal is not to have too much in savings for too long, but you will always have some unsold merchandise.

Keeping Records

To effectively operate your crafts business, you need to keep an accurate and current record of each item you make. Your inventory records should tell you:

- what the product was
- when it was made
- where it is now (not sold, in a consignment shop, etc.)
- how much it cost to make
- where you sold it
- when you sold it
- the price you sold it for
- your profit on that particular piece
- the total number of the same product sold thus far

This may seem like a tall order, but a simple index card file will do the trick in the early stages of your business. As your inventory grows, you may find it easier to keep track of your inventory in an inexpensive accounting ledger book.

You will find it easier to track extensive inventory using a computer with a simple database or spreadsheet program. If you already have a home computer, you can put it to good use keeping your inventory list up to date. But don't rush out and buy a computer just for this purpose. Just find a simple, convenient way to record the necessary information so you can refer to it.

Keeping accurate inventory records is very important. If you know which products sell best, you can make more of them. When you have a lot of product, it is easy to lose track. Once you have developed a system of your own, you will find that it really doesn't take much time. And the information you accumulate—even over a short period of time—will show you that it is well worth the effort.

Handle With Care

Since inventory is an investment in time and money, you should treat your inventory with great care.

When I am not actively selling, my products are stored safely and neatly. I store my fabric products loosely in boxes. They are always carefully covered to avoid dust and other debris and stored away from moisture and excessive heat.

The constant packing and unpacking, loading and unloading, from one show to another takes its toll on your carefully created merchandise. Ceramic, pottery and glass pieces risk being chipped with each packing and unpacking. Fabric items tend to wrinkle easily, and the more you iron them, the more they lose their "fresh" just-made look. Wood products can suffer chips and dents the more they are moved around.

When you pack for a show, try not to overcrowd your car. You don't want fabric products that look like you've slept on them, florals that look crushed and flat, wood that is scraped or dented, clay pieces that are chipped.

Inventory kept too long on the shelf can look old quickly. Also, many customers will probably handle your products before they decide to purchase them. This too takes its toll.

Try to price your products so you make a good profit, but don't price them so high that they remain too long on the shelf before being sold. Don't give your products a chance to get old or worn. Make them and move them out as quickly as possible.

Managing Your Stock

Good stock management, along with good inventory control, will help you make the most of the products on hand. How much inventory you will need to keep depends largely on how seriously and actively you pursue the selling aspect of your business. If you want to sell on many levels, you must be ready to restock a store, ship a mail order, and still gauge how much stock you will need for that craft show next weekend. You don't want to be caught short.

On the other hand, excessive stock breeds its own problems. Do you have room to keep a large inventory? Can you afford to tie up your money in a large amount of unsold product?

If you sell through stores, set up a rotating stock policy so you can move stock around among the different stores. Then if you need something from a store's stock to fill an order, it won't seem unusual to go to the store and change your stock.

Your inventory records can help you manage your stock—and help your sales.

In the beginning you will have no inventory history to work with, but pay attention to what sells and where it sells. Keep detailed records. After a selling pattern is established, your inventory history will help you see which products sold and which ones stayed in inventory too long before they were sold.

You can stop producing the less popular products and focus your attention and energy on the products that sell best. Since you will be constantly adding to and refining your product line, you will still need to monitor your new products closely. Also, people's tastes change from year to year. Your inventory history can help alert you to these changes in trends so you will be more prepared to meet them with a competitive product line.

Insurance

The saying "better safe than sorry" applies here. You need insurance. If you are crafting full time, you should make sure that your health-care needs are taken care of. If you have a large inventory, make sure you are covered if anything happens to that inventory. If you participate in craft shows and your products could possibly harm someone (even through misuse), you need to guard against potential lawsuits. The question of what type of insurance and how much coverage you will need can best be answered by your insurance agent.

Health Insurance

If you are in business full time, and you are not covered by your spouse's or any other insurance policy, you should investigate your medical and dental insurance options. Many crafters ignore this issue until it is too late. Though it may be costly, health insurance coverage is definitely worthwhile. If you are injured for an extended period of time, you won't make money from your crafts *and* you will be depleting your ready cash to pay medical bills.

Inventory and Equipment Insurance

You may not need this while your business is still small, but if you have a lucrative crafts business with lots of stock and expensive equipment, you need to protect it. There are insurance policies to protect your product and equipment or you may be able to add a rider to your current homeowner's or renter's policy for a nominal fee.

Suppose you're at a craft show and a gust of wind smashes all of your pottery to the ground. Could you afford to buy the raw materials to remake all your inventory? Suppose a power surge "zapped" your equipment. Would you have the money to replace it? I have seen these things happen. It's better to be prepared.

Personal Injury Insurance

If you participate in craft shows (and even if you don't), you might want to consider personal injury liability insurance.

If you demonstrate your craft at a show and use potentially dangerous equipment, there is always a risk of someone getting hurt. A soldering iron, a wood saw, even a glue gun, is a potential hazard. Someone who gets cut on the sharp edge of one of your products might sue you for medical expenses—and who knows what else. If you have a private showing at home and a customer trips and falls, you could be held liable. If a small child swallows a button "eye" from one of your dolls, you may be held responsible for any injury to that child. If your tent breaks loose on a windy day at a craft show and injures someone, you could be held liable.

I have firsthand experience with this one. Through no negligence on my part, the metal structure of a very sturdy pole tent tore in excessive wind. Someone got hurt and I was responsible. Fortunately, my insurance paid the $4,500 in medical bills.

These examples are not meant to discourage you—they are real possibilities for which you should prepare yourself. The monthly premium is definitely worth it for your peace of mind. Your insurance agent can give you sound advice on how to protect yourself.

Banking

How you set up your business says a lot about how you plan to approach this new venture.

If you use your regular personal checking account for your business as well as your personal expenses, you send a message to yourself that says, "I'm just trying this but I don't expect to be very successful." If you don't expect to succeed, you probably won't. If you open a separate checking account, the message becomes "I'm planning to take myself and this business seriously. I'll work as hard as I can and to this end, I will establish myself with a company account." This shows sincerity and a level of commitment. And if you take your business seriously, everyone will take your business seriously. See the difference?

So think carefully about this new venture. It's alright to be cautious, but your level of success will probably be in direct proportion to the level of your commitment.

You must open this second checking account for another very good reason—to monitor and segregate what you spend from what you make in your crafts business. This is very important for new crafters who tend to "forget" about small purchases.

Also, in the beginning, new crafters tend to overspend for supplies and raw materials, buying much more than they really need.

Having a separate account will teach you to discipline yourself. You won't spend unnecessarily. You will be able to see at a glance where your money has gone, so you can adjust your spending habits before you do serious damage to your profit margin. You will also be able to see clearly if you have really made any profits. You will have a record of every purchase made for your business. The bank fees on this account are deductible as part of the "cost of doing business."

There are three types of checking accounts you can set up for a crafts business:
- a second personal checking account
- a DBA ("doing business as") account
- a business checking account that requires a federal identification number

Personal Checking Account

You can just open a second personal checking account in your name. This only requires your social security number and a small opening deposit. You don't even need a business name.

I suggest ordering checks and a checkbook cover in a color different from your personal checks, so you won't make the mistake of writing personal checks for business expenses or paying for personal expenses from your business account.

DBA Account

A DBA ("doing business as") account is nothing more than a personal checking account with your company name added. You open the account under your own name with a second address line that reads "DBA Your Company Name."

This type of account is usually handled just like your personal checking account—check with your bank to be sure. If so, it can be opened with just your social security number and is subject to the same bank fees, regulations and restrictions as your personal checking account. The checks you deposit go through the same clearing process as those on your personal account. And, of course, you need a small deposit to initiate the account.

Having your business name on your checks will make you *feel* more professional. It will also make you appear more professional when dealing with suppliers, show promoters and the like. The DBA account is a good middle-of-the-road choice and the one that most new crafters use.

Business Account

A true business account requires a federal identification number that you obtain from the Department of the Treasury/Internal Revenue Service. This number is used instead of your social security number to open your business account.

Fees, charges, restrictions and regulations for a business account vary from bank to bank and may vary from your personal checking account. Some banks, for example, require you to use a portfolio-type checkbook that has a stub for every check.

Also, ask your bank how deposits are credited. They may be handled slightly differently from other types of accounts. This varies from bank to bank.

Using Your Separate Checking Account

Having a separate checking account—no matter which type you choose—will give you the best control over what is going on in your business. You can see at a glance how much money you are spending and how much (or little) profit you are realizing. It will also be much easier for you to summarize your business's activities if all the information is in one place. Be specific when you write entries in the check register and save all your receipts. Write down all of the particulars while the information is still at hand. Names, check numbers, amounts, descriptions, and explanations of unusual purchases are all important.

Use your company checkbook whenever you make a purchase for your business— no matter how small. Also, obtain a receipt when buying *anything* for your business. You must have receipts to substantiate expenses if you are ever audited by the IRS.

If you pay cash for any business purchase, get a receipt and pay yourself back by company check. If you make several small purchases (staples, magazines, straight pins, tape, etc.), keep the receipts together in an envelope and pay yourself back when it amounts to a reasonable sum. Make a note of what you purchased on each receipt. Be specific and enter all of the particulars in your check register when you write the check to yourself.

These small, seemingly insignificant expenses add up quickly and may make the difference between profit and loss. You need to keep track of them to get a realistic picture of what you are spending and how your business is doing.

Allocate a reasonable amount of money for initial expenses. Estimate what you will need to get started, and deposit that amount when you open your checking account. It doesn't have to be a lot, maybe $100 or so. Use this money to purchase raw materials while you are experimenting with your new craft ideas. Use it to pay for your tax certificate. Use it to buy instructional books on your chosen craft. Use it to pay for a craft class or two.

You should keep out-of-pocket expenses to a minimum until you start to sell. Equipment—if you will be using any type of machine—can be expensive. Don't buy top-of-the-line equipment for a craft that you are not sure you will like—or that will sell. Start with a basic, simple machine (maybe even a used one) until you have decided on your medium and craft. You may have to make additional out-of-pocket deposits to your account for equipment but set up a budget. Be frugal. Price shop and compare.

A sample page from a crafter's check register is shown on page 68. Notice how quickly the initial deposit was depleted. This is a good lesson in learning to watch your pennies.

Also notice how detailed each item is. That's the way it should be. The crafter can refer to the check register at any time and know everything there is to know about her business.

Notice the heading "my code." Obviously, there is no such column in any check register, but you should make one. Use an existing column or note your codes at the side of each page. Each expenditure should be categorized by a code. This will come in very handy at tax time. When you add up the totals for each code category, you will have a total picture of your business expenses. And you will have already done 95 percent of the accounting work necessary to file your tax return. You see? It's easy—simply a matter of detailed and accurate record keeping. I'll discuss the code categories in the section titled "The IRS and You" later in this chapter.

Sales Tax

There is a lot of misguided thinking among new crafters about sales tax. Let me explain. If you sell retail in a state, you must collect *that state's* sales tax. The tax must then be given back to the state in which you are selling. This means you need to apply for a sales tax certificate to obtain a sales tax number for *each state* in which you sell your products.

Each state has different sales tax laws. Some don't collect sales tax on children's clothing. Others only tax clothing items of $75 or more per item. States have different tax percentages—6%, 7.5%, etc.

Some very large cities have an additional city tax, and some areas have a county sales tax. These are things that you should know before selling in each new area. It is your responsibility to research the tax laws before selling in a new location. Often, the show promoter will have this information. Also, individual city and state departments will be glad to answer your questions—just call and ask!

Start by selling in your own state, just to get the feel of it before branching out

CHECK REGISTER

CHECK NUMBER	CHECK DATE	DESCRIPTION OF TRANSACTION	(-) PAYMENT/DEBIT	My code	(+) DEPOSIT/CREDIT	BALANCE 400.00
001	1/3/95	Mary Jane's Sewing Shop				
		Singer sewing machine Model No. MERIT 270				
		Serial No. 54455335621 $125.00		E	(for "equipment")	
		6 bobbins $4.25/ 4 needles $2.50		S	(for "supplies)	
		subtotal $131.75 tax (7%) $9.22	140.97			259.03
002	1/5/95	State of CT - Revenue Svcs	20.00	L	(for "license")	239.03
003	1/10/95	Barnes & Noble Bookstore				
		"_____" magazine $2.95				
		"_____" magazine $1.79				
		"How to start a Business" book $14.95				
		subtotal $19.69 tax(7%) $1.39	21.08	S	(for supplies)	217.95
004	1/15/95	Carter's Office Supply				
		stapler $11.00/staples $1.89				
		index cards $1.19/pens&pencils $2.95				
		subtotal $17.03 tax(7%) $1.19	18.22	OFC	(for"office")	199.73
005	1/20/95	Northern Press				
		business cards $29.00 tax(7%) $2.03	31.03	A	(for"advertising")	168.70
006	1/20/95	Fabco Fabric Shop				
		4 yds. calico @2.95/$11.80 tx(7%)83¢	12.63	RM	(for "raw materials")	156.07
					and so on...	

This sample check register will give you an idea of just how valuable this little book can be when tax time comes. Just add up the different categories in the "my code" column and you will have done 95 percent of the work that you need to do to file your tax return.

into different states and applying for multiple tax numbers. Remember, if you have a myriad of tax numbers, you will have to file reports for each of those states. Some require quarterly filing, others require annual filing. Decide where you want to sell before you apply to the state for a tax number.

Your state and an adjoining state may have "combined" tax certificates that allow you to file in your home state for sales made in both that state and an adjoining state. Your state then forwards the revenue due to the other state. Again, check with your state tax office for more information on this type of tax certificate.

Some people mistakenly think that sales tax is cutting into their profits. The tax money that you return to the state is not taken from your profits—it is added to your selling price. You are not losing money. You are just collecting tax and giving it to the government.

Applying for a Sales Tax Number

You request an application by calling the tax department in your state. Note: This is *not* the IRS—it is a *state* agency. Some states charge a nominal fee ($20 or so) for processing your application. Some states don't charge anything. Some only charge out-of-state merchants.

When you apply for a sales tax number, allow plenty of time for the processing. It can take three months or more. Apply early just to be safe. Also, send the application by certified mail. It is not expensive and you'll have proof that the application arrived.

Most craft show promoters ask for your sales tax number on the show application. They are not responsible for enforcing state codes, but in most cases they are requested by the state to send a list of all participating crafters for each event. Some promoters refuse applications with no sales tax number unless you are selling an item that isn't taxable.

State inspectors regularly visit craft shows and impose fines if you do not have the proper licensing. To avoid problems, get a sales tax certificate.

Benefits of a Sales Tax Number

Having a sales tax number has its advantages. It enables you to buy raw materials without paying sales tax at the time of purchase—even at your local stores. This is because *you* will collect the sales tax on the finished product when you sell it to the *final* customer.

With a sales tax number you can also buy your raw materials wholesale directly from manufacturers and distributors rather than going to your local store and paying their markup. When buying raw materials, you must present a copy of your sales tax certificate to the supplier. The supplier will keep the copy on record and not charge you sales tax on your purchases.

Note: You do not pay sales tax when you purchase raw materials that you will incorporate into your finished products. But when you buy office supplies, equipment, magazines, etc., you *do* pay applicable sales tax since you will not be reselling them—*you* are the end user.

Collecting Sales Tax

When you receive your sales tax certificate, you will also receive a tax rate chart to use for calculating tax on individual sales.

Many crafters include the sales tax in the price of the finished product. Then they "back it out" and send a check to the state when they are doing their accounting. This eliminates the need to calculate and add tax on each individual sale or piece as it is sold. Including the tax in the finished product price and then rounding the price off to the nearest dollar also eliminates the need for you to carry coins—quarters, nickels, dimes and pennies. Just remember to calculate the sales tax on the original price of the product, not the price that includes the tax.

If you sell wholesale (that is, to someone who will resell your product), you do not charge sales tax. Again, sales tax is charged on the *final* retail sale only. This may sound tricky, but just remember—the *end user* (*final* purchaser) pays the tax. If you aren't selling to the end user, you don't collect sales tax.

At some craft shows, participants do not collect any money from customers. You fill out sales slips and give one to each customer. The customer makes her selections from you and from the other crafters at the show, collecting sales slips as she goes along. When she is finished making her selections, she pays for all of her purchases at one time directly to the organization sponsoring the show. The organization collects the payments, deducts their commission, and pays the crafters at the end of the day. In this case the organization is the one selling to the end user. If any tax is to be collected, the organization should collect it and report it to the state.

If you ever participate in this type of show, you will find some crafters collecting tax anyway. They shouldn't be. They do this to recoup some of the commission they are giving to the sponsoring organization. Be fair. It's not worth the risk to your reputation.

Reporting Sales Tax

When you receive your tax certificate, information will be enclosed explaining what is taxable and what is not.

Reporting the taxes you've collected is relatively simple. The states usually send you their forms—some quarterly and some annually—and as long as you keep accurate records, it is easy to file a return and pay the state its due. The forms themselves are simple.

Many crafters open a separate savings account to keep the sales tax they collect until it is time to pay the state. If you keep the state's money separate, you won't be tempted to spend it. After all, it was never really yours to spend.

Accepting Payment

Sales are very important. You want to sell as much product as you can. To do this, you must be able to accept as many forms of payment as your customers will want to use. Though many customers will pay you in cash, some will want to write a personal check. Still others will prefer paying by credit card. You should be prepared to accept all these forms of payment.

Cash Sales

Cash transactions are my favorite. I see it as immediate gratification for a job well done. And when you make a cash sale, the transaction is final once you hand over the product to the customer and receive payment. Many customers will pay in cash, especially for moderate- to low-priced items.

But what if your products are more expensive or if the customer doesn't have enough cash to purchase the items she wishes to buy?

Payment by Personal Check

Personally, I have been very lucky and have never received a bad check from a customer. I know other crafters who have not been so fortunate.

This is not to say that there are a rash of people frequenting craft shows and writing bad checks. This is far from true. But when you accept a personal check as payment, you are taking a small risk.

Here are some guidelines to help you avoid getting into the collections business when accepting personal checks:

- Never accept a check that doesn't have the person's name and street address preprinted at the top.
- Get the person's phone number.
- Always ask for a second form of identification with a picture and signature—like a driver's license. Record the license number and state on the check.
- Check to see that the address on the license matches the address on the check.

Don't let this list discourage you. Personal checks are very much an accepted form of payment at craft shows. Just take the few precautions listed.

Credit Card Sales

Some customers prefer to pay for purchases by credit card. Accepting payment by credit card can *significantly* increase your sales.

Getting initial approval to accept credit cards from the major credit card companies is not always easy for a "transient" vendor. You have no formal business address since you work from your home. But with many successful home businesses in operation today, the credit card companies have relaxed their rules a bit. Check with your bank first. If you have a good credit record with them, they may be able to help you.

You don't need to accept *all* major credit cards, but you should be able to accept at least one of them. If you can get approval for more than one, that's great.

I accept only the American Express Card and its affiliates. Why? Because American Express approved my application and I have never found a reason to apply to the other major credit card companies. I have never lost a sale because American Express was the only card I accepted. Apply to several companies and hope that at least one of them will approve your application.

Remember that this service is not free. For each sale you make using a credit card, you have to pay a percentage of the sale to the credit card company. And there is a delay, usually one or two weeks, in receiving payment.

Also, you have to get approval for each sale from the credit card company. You do this by phone. You will have to go to a phone and call in each sale to get approval. Some crafters don't call in each sale. They wait until the end of the day and call in all their credit card sales at once. This does save time, but it's risky. What do you do if someone isn't approved? The customer has already gone home with your product.

In spite of these complications, it is definitely in your best interest to get approval from at least one major credit card company. Often, sales of expensive items or of multiple items would never be made if the customers couldn't pay by credit card.

I can't tell you how many times a sale has been doubled—or more—once the customer realized I accept a credit card. I have also had cases where a customer couldn't decide between two products and purchased *both* of them because they could pay by credit card.

If you intend to do any mail-order business, you *must* get approval to accept at least one card. In this case, the more credit cards you can accept the better.

The IRS and You

As a business, you must report your income to the IRS and pay taxes on it. The forms are simple and the logic is clear. You complete a "Schedule C—Profit or Loss from Business" form and submit this along with your other tax documents to the IRS each April.

Schedule C is not a long form. It fills both sides of one sheet of paper. That's all. It is divided into four parts:

- Basic information (name, address, business type, social security number, etc.)
- Income (sales)
- Expenses (advertising, commissions, fees, office expenses, licenses, etc.)
- Cost of goods sold (inventory, manufacturing materials, production supplies)

This is where accurate record keeping comes in. If you have clearly documented your income, tracked your expenses, and kept a current inventory list, then you should have no trouble completing this form. Simply put, it's a matter of adding up your sales, then deducting your allowable expenses and reconciling your inventory balance or cash from year to year.

Look back at the sample check register. Now look at a current year's Schedule C. The codes and categories that you set up to identify your expenses and other items in your check register should correspond to the line items listed on the Schedule C. Just add up each code and place the total on the corresponding line of the Schedule C. That's all there is to it!

Here is a short list of expenses that can be deducted on Schedule C, just to give you an idea. The forms may change from year to year so I have not included a copy of an actual Schedule C in this book. It's best to work with a current copy.

- Advertising
- Bad debt (bad checks, etc.)
- Car and truck expenses (business use of your vehicle)

PETER STONE—
CANVAS PRODUCTS

Peter Stone is a different kind of craftsperson. He doesn't sell his products in stores, and he doesn't go to craft shows. Peter's products are custom-made and fitted to the customer's specifications. He makes canvas boat covers. And he makes a lot of them. With nearby Candlewood Lake beckoning boat enthusiasts from all over, Peter has found his niche.

Though Peter is not a "traditional crafter," he still lives by the same rules as other crafters. He is required to have a state sales tax number. He files the same type of tax return we do—using the Schedule C.

His first craft job was as a part-time apprentice for an upholstery and boat cover shop in New Milford, Connecticut. That was in 1958. He worked there for two years and learned how to measure and fit boat covers for any type of boat—and he learned how to sew.

Then other aspects of his life took him away from canvas work for several years. But not forever. Peter was smart and recognized a profitable business when he saw one. So eventually he returned to the same upholstery shop, rented a space of his own, and bought some of their equipment to set up his own business making boat covers.

Though he still worked only part time, his business was successful and in 1985 he bought and renovated a commercial building in New Milford to house his canvas business and his other love—antique cars. From spring through autumn, the boat cover business is very busy. When winter comes and the boat business slows down, he makes and fits truck bed covers. So he is busy all year 'round.

Peter Stone still works only part-time at his canvas business but he says, "It's something that I enjoy and having a profitable second business allows me to support my other hobbies and enjoy some of the finer things in life."

- Commissions and fees
- Depreciation (of business equipment)
- Insurance (not health insurance—business related only)
- Interest (on loans for your business)
- Legal and professional services (accounting, etc.)
- Office expense (stationery, stamps, business cards, computer supplies, etc.)
- Rent or lease (business only)
- Repairs and maintenance (of business equipment, etc.)
- Supplies (other miscellaneous expenses)
- Taxes and licenses (cost of getting your state sales tax number, etc.)
- Travel, meals and entertainment (expense of going to a show, visiting a store, etc.)
- Utilities (phone, electric, etc., specifically related to your business)

You may want to enlist the advice of an accountant or tax consultant, especially for the "expenses" part. A good accountant can save you money. Tax laws are constantly being revised, and a good accountant knows best which expense deductions are currently allowed and which are not.

If you don't want to bear the expense of hiring an accountant, you *can* do this yourself. (I've done it for years and I haven't been audited yet!)

In addition to Schedule C, you may also be required to file a Schedule SE for social security self-employment tax. Even if you do have an accountant handle your tax filing, you should still be familiar with these forms, the data required to complete them, and the basic tax rules for running a home business. Call your local tax office and request copies of these forms so you'll know what information you will need and how best to organize it for your taxes and your check register.

Here are a few of the useful IRS publications, available free at any IRS office:

- Publication 538 "Accounting Periods and Methods"
- Publication 334 "Tax Guide for Small Business"
- Publication 535 "Business Expense"
- Publication 463 "Travel, Entertainment and Gift Expenses"
- Publication 533 "Self-Employment Tax"
- Publication 560 "Retirement Plans for the Self-Employed"
- Publication 583 "Taxpayers Starting a Business"
- Publication 587 "Business Use of Your Home"
- Publication 917 "Business Use of a Car"

Hobby vs. Business

If you don't eventually make a profit, if you do not keep accurate records of income and expenses, have a separate checking account, save expense receipts, etc., then the IRS might decide that what you have is an expensive *hobby* and not a business at all. This is not always bad. In some cases, it may even work to your advantage to call it a hobby.

But if you want to qualify as a business, you should show a profit at least three out of five years. This is a sobering thought. Of course, in your first year at least, you may show a loss because of equipment and material purchases. You'll spend a lot on raw materials and new equipment in an effort to build your inventory, and you may not sell much product. In this case, a loss filing is inevitable. But eventually you must show a profit or at least a very serious *intent* to make a profit.

The "Professionals"

Once you're off to a good start you'll want to learn more about making your business a success. Certain professionals can help. Take the time to seek them out and ask questions.

An accountant can offer you valuable information and sound advice on how to organize your accounting books, how to keep records of expenses and profit, which charges are tax deductible and which are not. He or she can also advise you on keeping inventory records. Your accountant will tell you what records will be needed to prepare your taxes at the end of the year.

Do not wait until the end of the year to consult a professional. Start now. The more you know in advance about the business end of running your business, the better off you will be, financially and otherwise.

Your insurance agent can protect you, your product, your equipment, and, most of all, your peace of mind. Find out what types of coverage are available and how much they cost. Ask what policies would benefit you and your business.

You may not want to take advantage of all that is offered. Or initially, you may not be able to afford to. But it never hurts to have the informaton you need to make educated decisions.

Also, it wouldn't hurt to read a good book on "small business" or "home business." There are some very good ones available. Skim through a few and select the ones that you find easiest to follow. It won't do any good if you can't understand them. I recommend the fifth edition of *Homemade Money* by Barbara Brabec (Betterway

Books). It's a gold mine of information about every aspect of successfully running a business at home.

Many schools and colleges offer small-business seminars or courses. Check into it and take at least one. It's time and money well spent.

There is a lot to learn about the business of running even a small business. The more you know, the easier it becomes, and the better your business will be. You can do it. Learning anything new does take some time and adjustment. Really, an hour or two a week may be all you need to dedicate to the paperwork of your business. You may even find this time a welcome break from crafting.

With a minimum of fuss you'll be able to relegate the time that you spend ''businessing'' to only a small fraction of your total time. And you can spend the rest of your time doing what you like best—making and selling your crafts.

CHAPTER WORKSHEET

Managing the business side of selling your crafts is not difficult. All it takes is a little organization in the beginning and a bit of discipline to maintain good work habits after. This worksheet will help you get started and help you track your progress.

Inventory

I will keep my inventory history:

on my home computer

on index cards

in an accounting ledger book

other _____

Banking

I opened a separate checking account today. Date _____

My Budget

My initial deposit of $ _____ will be used to pay for: Amount Allocated

a sales tax certificate   _____

magazines   _____

instructional craft books   _____

a book on small business management   _____

a craft class   _____

a subscription to a craft show listings publication   _____

office supplies   _____

equipment   _____

TOTAL $ _____

Raw Materials I need to get started: Amount Allocated

_____   _____

_____   _____

_____   _____

_____   _____

_____   _____

_____   _____

_____   _____

TOTAL $ _____

Insurance

I asked my insurance agent about the following insurance policies and coverage:

Annual Cost:

Health insurance $_____

Replacement insurance for inventory and equipment $_____

Personal injury and liability insurance $_____

Sales Tax

I called my state tax office for a sales tax application on _____ (date)

I returned the sales tax application on _____ (date)

I received my sales tax certificate on _____ (date)

My sales tax number is _____

My sales tax certificate expires on _____ (date)

Accepting Payment for My Crafts

I have applied to the following credit card companies for approval:

Name	Date	Accepted	
_____	_____	Yes	No
_____	_____	Yes	No
_____	_____	Yes	No

The IRS and You

I will use the following checkbook category codes to designate expenses (see page 73 for more details):

Advertising	_____	Rent or lease	_____
Bad debt	_____	Repairs/Maintenance	_____
Car/Vehicle business use	_____	Supplies	_____
Commissions & Fees	_____	Taxes and Licenses	_____
Insurance	_____	Travel, meals & entertainment	_____
Interest	_____	Utilities	_____
Legal & Professional Services	_____	Raw Materials	_____
Office expense	_____	Other	_____

CHAPTER FIVE

THE THREE Ps IN PROFIT

OK. Now that you have chosen your craft and medium, defined your product line, listed the products in that product line, set up a system for tracking your inventory, opened a checking account, made insurance arrangements, applied for a sales tax number, and done some research on your taxes and what the IRS expects of you, you should be ready to get on with some of the really interesting issues so important to making a success of your crafts—purchasing raw materials, producing inventory and pricing your products.

So far you have incurred expenses, but you haven't made any *profit*. As with any new business, these initial expenses and hidden costs can't be avoided. Hopefully, you have been cautious and frugal and any supplies that you bought while experimenting with your ideas haven't cost you too much money.

You will reap the best rewards if you pay attention to the "three Ps" in profit:

• Purchase raw materials economically.

• Produce your products efficiently.

• Price your products effectively.

Never try to increase your profit margin by decreasing the quality of your products. Handmade quality—more than anything else—is what a crafter sells and what a craft customer wants to buy. You might try to make a product simpler but never cheaper.

Every unnecessary dollar you spend on supplies and each extra minute you spend on production affects your bottom line—your profit. So you need to examine all costs carefully and determine which expenses are necessary, which can be reduced, and which can be eliminated or at least postponed until you start receiving some income.

Purchasing Supplies

Making smart purchasing choices will go a long way toward increasing your profits. Knowing when it is best to purchase wholesale and knowing when to buy retail is an important key.

Buying Retail

At first, you will probably buy your supplies directly from a retailer. Since you will be buying in small quantities, that's OK. Once you get your sales tax certificate, remember to submit a copy to each store you patronize so you won't have to pay sales tax on your raw materials.

Once you have decided on your basic product line and have made a few products, you will have a good idea what raw materials you will need. You may not know exact quantities, but you won't know that until you start selling. You won't have a great deal of money either. So start small, but as soon as you get your tax certificate consider making your first wholesale purchase.

Buying Wholesale

There comes a time when every new crafter considers buying supplies on a larger scale. This is good! It means that you are secure enough in your craft and your product line to make a commitment. These larger stock purchases should *not* be made at a retail store. It is time to contact a manufacturer or distributor and buy wholesale.

Do start buying wholesale as soon as possible but don't overbuy. Often a bulk shipment from a manufacturer is not much more material than you would normally purchase from your local supplier. And the "bulk" doesn't always mean buying all of one product either. You can usually purchase a total order of several items from the same wholesaler.

Buying wholesale is easier than you think and you will be amazed at the savings—usually about half of what it would cost retail. Think how your profits will increase!

Although some manufacturers only sell to "storefronts" and won't deal with a home

LORRAINE O' DONNELL—THE SILK FLOWER LADY

Lorraine O'Donnell is a floral crafter who specializes in silk flowers. Silk flowers are not as fragile as dried flowers and last longer. Her display consists of many wonderful and original floral creations.

Lorraine has the right idea about pricing, too. Her products are priced to sell. To do this, she buys her raw materials in quantity at a wholesale level. She also produces her most popular pieces in larger batches to save on labor. This gives her the opportunity to pass some of her savings along to her customers. Her products are by no means cheap, but they are reasonably priced. She still makes a good profit and customers are happy to be able to afford to purchase her lovely florals.

Lorraine also has a wide variety of products, from small bathroom pieces to very elaborate wreaths and table arrangements. That is probably why she is so successful. (Of course, her winning smile and her warm personality could also have a little bit to do with it.)

She is also a very good salesperson. She doesn't crowd the customer, but she is always available to explain a piece, find a color that the customer requested, or do whatever she can to help a customer make a purchase. And that is the key. You are not there to convince the customer to make a purchase—you are just there to help them make a purchase. And reasonable prices are the surest way I know of to do that.

business, this attitude is rapidly evaporating in the 1990s. Merchants are beginning to recognize the potential of the home business market and cater to it.

The more cautious manufacturers will deal with you only if you have been in business for a few years. That's OK. Don't be discouraged. Many major companies (you'll be surprised at who and how many) will gladly do business with you. All you need to do is ask.

They will probably want credit references to open an account and you may have to place a substantial first order ($100 to $300) and possibly pay for it in advance. It's worth it. Thereafter, most companies will accept smaller orders, though some companies have a standing "minimum order" policy. Each company is different.

Do a little self-examination before you make any large wholesale purchases. Ask yourself:

- How much material do I really need?
- How much money will I save?
- Is it worth tying up a larger sum of money to establish a business relationship with a maufacturer?
- How long will it take me to use this shipment?
- How many pieces of product can I make from this?
- If I buy this shipment, how much more profit per piece will I make?
- Do I have enough space to store what I will not immediately use?
- Am I sure that the products I will make from it will sell?
- Am I sure that I will ultimately use all that I am purchasing?

Don't weigh yourself down with large bills and huge shipments until you are sure you have selected a craft and product line that will work and will sell well for you.

Finding Suppliers

When you have an item that you would like to purchase in bulk, play detective! Find the source. Call the manufacturer directly. The company name and location should be written on any product packaging. If not, there is usually some information available on the packaging. Also, a number of suppliers are listed at the end of chapter two.

Here are ways you can research additional sources of your raw materials:

- Call the 800 directory operator at (800) 555-1212. If the company has a toll-free number, the operator will give it to you.
- If you have a city name but no 800 number, get the city's area code and call the information operator at (area code) 555-1212.
- If just the state name is listed, you may have to try the information operator for

each area code in that state. The area codes are listed in your local telephone book.

- Go to your local library and consult *The Thomas Register*, a directory of manufacturers listed by manufacturer name and by product.
- Ask another crafter who uses the same products.
- Write to the editor of a national craft magazine for information.
- Buy *The Crafts Supply Sourcebook* edited by Margaret Boyd (Betterway Books) at your local bookstore.

There is always a way to find the source. A crafter friend of mine found a supplier of gift boxes for her products in an unusual way.

While Elizabeth was driving she saw a truck go by that mentioned "gift boxes" on the side. She followed the truck until she could write down the name and telephone number of the company. Then she called the company directly, spoke with a salesperson, got a catalog and placed an order. Now she buys all her gift boxes from that company.

When you have the name and number of the manufacturer, call and ask for the sales department. Speak directly to a salesperson. Be professional and polite. Have an idea of *what* material and *how much* you want to purchase and know the retail selling price, if possible. The manufacturer's prices will be approximately half a retail store's price and should vary slightly depending on the quantity you purchase. Larger quantities can mean bigger discounts.

Ask for a catalog. The manufacturer may have other products and accessories you could use. Also, the catalog may give you some new ideas.

Some companies request a small payment for sample packets, fabric swatches or large wholesale catalogs. You will have to send a check before receiving any swatches, samples or catalogs. (Don't forget to use your *company* check!)

Ask the salesperson about the minimum order policy and about quantity price breaks and credit terms. They are in the business of selling so they will be happy to give you this information. Ask for a credit application.

Ask about COD shipments. There may be a time when you need a product in a rush. The company could send it COD the day you order it.

If the manufacturer will not sell to you directly, ask for the name of their distributor. This is the middle agent between the large manufacturer and the small retailer. Call the distributor and get the above information from them. Your discount may not be as high as from the manufacturer, but your minimum order should be considerably lower. Ask for a catalog or brochure, and ask what other product lines the distributor represents. You may find a good source for other raw materials you need.

In your quest for reasonably priced raw materials, don't ignore discount houses, "odd lot" stores, even flea markets! You can find many wonderful items at very reasonable prices. If the product is damaged, don't buy it. However, it may be a "one-time-deal" that can't be reordered, but it may still be a worthwhile purchase.

You should also find out when your craft stores and suppliers have their sales. If you have capital and storage space to spare, you can take advantage of after-season and preseason sales.

Getting the Most for Your Money

An example of the cost of raw materials for a real product will give you a good idea of how wholesale and discount purchasing can greatly increase your profits. Remember, these are *real* costs for a *real* product. The product? A 54-inch round Victorian Christmas tree skirt.

	Retail	*Wholesale*
	(no min. order)	(min. order 50 yds.)
1½ yds. fabric	$7.99/yd.	$3.99/yd.
Per Product	$11.99	$5.99
Total Purchase	$11.99	**$199.50**

Wholesale is the only way to buy the fabric. I can buy fifty yards total of the same fabric in different colors. That will make approximately thirty-three pieces of product. It is worth the initial $199.50 investment.

	Retail	*Wholesale*
	(no min. order)	(min. order $100)
5 yds. lace	$3.94/yd.	$0.99/yd.
Per Product	$19.70	$4.95
Total Purchase	$19.70	$100.00 (**$165.00**, see below)

Again, wholesale wins. I don't have to buy $100 worth of the same lace, just a total of $100 of a variety of different laces (minimum 25 yards per lace). In fact, since I am making thirty-three tree skirts, I will order about $165 worth of trim—enough for all of my tree skirts! Otherwise I would have to place another $100 minimum order later.

	Retail (no min. order)	Wholesale (min. order $150)	Fabric Store Sale (no min.)
½ yds. liner fabric	$4.99/yd.	$1.99/yd.	$0.99/yd.
Per Product	$7.49	$2.99	$1.49
Total Purchase	$4.50	$150.00	$200.00

I make a lot of this product, and I use the same liner in the same neutral color for most of them. No problem to spend $150.00 on it. *But* my local fabric store was having a sale. I found fabric of equal quality in the right color on sale for $0.99 per yard. They were overstocked and needed to sell some inventory. I knew I might never see so much of my fabric on sale for such a great price again. So I bought all they had—$200.00 worth!

	Retail (no min. order)	Wholesale (min. order 50 rolls assorted colors)
5 yds. ribbon	$0.50/10 yd. roll	$0.43/10 yd. roll
Per Product	$0.25 (½ roll)	$0.22
Total Purchase	$0.50	$21.50

The wholesale savings wasn't much greater than the sale price at my local fabric store. Also, the "assorted colors" didn't meet my needs. Ribbon is not an expensive item, and I have saved so much on my other materials that I can afford to be choosy about getting exactly the right shade.

Now, look at the difference!

Total Cost Per Product	
Retail	*My Cost*
$39.43	$12.68

The difference between retail and wholesale for the materials to make this product is $26.75! Yes, that's $26.75 more profit on just one item!

I also use thread for this product. Since it may vary in texture and color from product to product, I don't usually buy it wholesale. But I do buy it *on* sale. By planning my expenditures and not impulse buying, I get the most for my money.

Production

How you produce your product can also have a great impact on your profits. You should set up a production schedule and try to keep to it as much as possible. Plan your whole inventory, then schedule the time necessary to make each product.

Producing in Quantity

Making only one of a product is not cost-effective. Your "batch size" should be no fewer than five units, but it can be as many units as you are comfortable making at one time.

Don't get carried away, though—producing too large a batch can also cause problems. You might end up with one hundred pieces of unfinished product that you can't sell because you ran out of time rather than have five or ten pieces of finished product that you can sell.

As you discover what sells and what doesn't, you can adjust your production. Plan cautiously and don't make too many pieces of a product if you're not sure the product will sell. Even if you have initial success with a product, don't go crazy and make a hundred pieces. You may have them for a very long time.

Only after you have consistent *success with a product should you consider buying and producing in great quantities.*

Your initial five pieces of a product don't have to be all the same color, but the basic manufacturing process should be the same. Remember, time is money. Make the same product in different sizes. Cut different fabrics for several different items from the same pattern at the same time. Pour several different molds from the same batch of plaster.

Do you use one color of thread or paint for one process and another color for the next step? Don't waste time changing threads or paint pots after each piece. Sew what needs to be sewn with the same thread at the same time. Paint items of the same color at the same time. *Then* change and finish the pieces.

Buy extra bobbins and wind several at the same time so you won't have to stop in the middle of a piece because you ran out of bobbin thread. Have plenty of extra paint brushes. Cut wood pieces all together, then stain or paint them all at one time. Then cut some more while the first pieces are drying.

Because you have economized on your production time, you can sell for less and still make a higher profit on each item.

Production Planning

Planning is the key to successful and profitable production. Once you have decided on your main product line, think about what you will make first and second and third, how many you will make of each and in what colors. This planning will also help you plan your buying. You will not purchase raw materials unless and until you need them.

Planning will help you make the most of your time, efforts and materials. It will give you the best possible profit margin for your business. And this is what you want—profit.

Graduated Product Lines

Making larger products first and then incorporating your leftover materials into smaller products within the same product line theme is a very profitable method of production.

Once you start selling, especially at craft shows, you will see how these smaller items add significant dollars to your profits. And including smaller items will rid your work area of clutter.

These "bottom line" products are basically free items—ones that can be priced only for your labor and not for any cost of materials. If they are relatively simple and quick to make, you can keep the labor costs low. But remember—never sacrifice quality.

Motivation

Constant and consistent production can be tedious. Think of ways to make it fun. Make yourself happy while you work.

Every crafter has a device for staying motivated. Some play their favorite music while they work—and some even sing along (when nobody's listening). This is fine if it doesn't distract you.

Other crafters promise themselves a reward after a long production run. Or they give themselves a "prize" at the end of a particularly hectic workday if they meet their goals. It doesn't have to be much: a pint of Häagen-Dazs, a pizza out instead of cooking at home, a movie—anything that keeps you on track.

My motivation is simple—*money*. If I start a production run that will produce $400 worth of product, I mentally pay myself in stages for the work done. When I am one-fourth finished, I mentally pay myself $100. This doesn't seem like much money, so it motivates me to get at least one-half done—the $200 mark. Now we're talking bigger dollars. I want the whole $400. Before I realize it I have completed the batch, and I have mentally paid myself the full $400. Good job, Kathy!

Find the motivation that you need to keep producing. Your efforts will first pay off when you look at your display after you've set it up at a show. You'll be proud—as you will have every right to be. When customers *oooh* and *ahhh* over your wonderful products, you will be glad you took the time and care to produce them. When you start actually selling them, that's the best reward of all. It's one thing to be appreciated, but it is entirely another thing to be appreciated in dollars. You'll see.

Pricing

When you set a price on a product, you must be able to pay yourself a reasonable amount for labor, recoup your raw material costs, and cover any overhead and selling costs.

Don't ignore overhead expenses. They will definitely have an impact on your profit. Overhead expenses that new crafters might ignore are:

- Phone calls—to dealers, distributors, the information operator, show promoters, other crafters and customers (business-related calls only)
- Magazines, books, industry publication subscriptions, memberships, etc.
- Office supplies—paper, staples, index cards, accounting books, envelopes, etc.
- Postage—for show applications, letters and payments to salespeople, information sent to your customers, business bill payments
- Utilities—electricity, etc. (if you can substantiate an increase between your normal use and usage after you started your business)
- Car use and mileage—to the show, to the store
- Insurance (other than health insurance) for your business
- Licenses (such as your state sales tax license)
- Equipment maintenance and repair—dry-cleaning your table covers, machine servicing, etc.
- Rent or mortgage—for a room or area specifically and only used for your business
- Monthly bank fees and checks for your business account

Pricing competitively and making a good profit can be done. Some guidelines and a basic formula can be suggested, but only you know how much money you spent on raw materials and how much production time you spent on each item. Only you know

CHERYL NICKLAW—
A SUCCESS STORY

Cheryl Nicklaw is as successful a dried floral crafter as I've ever seen. She prices her products reasonably yet competitively and is always a huge success at craft shows. And you always know that most of what Cheryl brings to a show was just made, because she comes very close to selling all her inventory at her shows. In fact, Cheryl has to have additional help at her booth to keep up with the sales and interest that her products generate.

Cheryl's florals are original and traditional. The variety of product she brings to a show is positively astounding. She had to purchase a very long and large van to accommodate all of it!

your overhead expenses. Only you know what profit you need to make to be successful. Therefore, only you can set a selling price that enables you to recoup your expenses and make a reasonable profit. That is why it is so important to watch your spending; you have to get those dollars back somehow.

New crafters often set a price on a product without much rhyme or reason. They look at the finished product only at its face value, not at the whole cost picture. They set an emotional price but not a logical one. This is a grave mistake.

Pricing Too Low

Pricing too low is something a lot of new crafters do. In the beginning the excitement and the need to sell something they have made overwhelms them. They are so happy just to *sell* that they don't realize they are losing money until it's too late. Their logic is that, well, they enjoy making crafts and they don't care about the money. Not true. Everybody cares about money!

New crafters also tend to be very modest about the value of their work. But, somewhere down the road, when they are working like a fiend to produce more product and dipping into their own pocket for more money for supplies, they wonder: "If I am selling so well, why am I not making any money?"

Eventually, they become discouraged and give up their ideas altogether. What a shame. Their ideas may have been wonderful. But they didn't watch their spending, they didn't monitor the time spent making their products, they didn't watch their income and make sure that it justified their time and expenses. They watched the crafting but not the bottom line.

Pricing a product too low can also turn off prospective buyers. If they feel you value your work too little, they may do the same. One of the product lines I produced over the years was a line of dolls. I made dolls to match various decors, with decorator fabric dresses, hats and flower baskets. They sold very well. Except for one doll that was dressed in gold satin. Personally, I hated the doll after it was made. I took it to the first show. It didn't sell. In fact, no one even looked at it. So, at the next show, I priced it $5.00 lower than the other dolls. My first customer looked at the doll, saw the price tag and asked, "What's wrong with this one?" I told her that nothing was wrong with the doll. She didn't buy it.

The next customer who showed an interest in the doll asked the same question. I told her that the fabric was slightly less expensive than the fabrics used on the other dolls (which it was). She didn't buy the doll either. After a whole day of answering the same question, I rethought my approach.

The following day at the same show, I priced that doll $5.00 *higher* than the others. The first customer who came in that morning picked up the doll in the shiny satin dress, didn't ask why it was priced higher and bought it. Who can figure?

Pricing Too High

Pricing a product too high is just as easy to do and just as fatal a mistake. Keep in mind that once you get the hang of production, it won't take you as long to make your finished products as it did to make the first few of each design. As you progress you will streamline your production line. You will find new ways to use your scraps.

Also bear in mind that your profit margin won't be the same on every piece. Some pieces will take less time to produce and, therefore, cost you less in labor. Others may use less expensive materials. Still others may use more expensive materials and more time. You will have to price these items higher, so you might have to settle for a smaller profit margin. If they are consistent sellers, though, you may want to continue making them.

This is not to say that you shouldn't make as much profit as possible on each piece. If your raw materials didn't cost too much, if it didn't take you long to make the product, and you can *still* sell it for a high price, then by all means do so. Try to be realistic, but whatever the market will bear is what you should ultimately sell your product for.

Effective Pricing—Wholesale

There is a fine line between pricing your products too high and too low. A simple rule for calculating a product's wholesale price is to multiply the raw materials by a minimum of two times their cost and then add at least $10 an hour in labor. This is an extremely oversimplified formula. It depends on whether or not your overhead and selling costs can be covered by the "two times the raw materials" rule.

Some crafters multiply their material costs by three to leave a wider margin to cover overhead and selling expenses. Others pay themselves $12 to $15 per hour. But these formulas are just ways to get a ballpark figure for a wholesale price. Then you can adjust it.

In setting a wholesale price, the cost of materials is only one of many considerations. Your wholesale price should cover the cost of raw materials, overhead, labor, and the cost of selling. And still leave you with a good profit margin and capital to work with.

Depending on your methods of selling, the cost of selling may include any one or more of the followng:

- Craft shows—fees, display equipment, credit card equipment and processing
- Salespeople—commission (usually 15 to 25 percent of wholesale price), samples
- Consignment shops—commission (10 to 60 percent of retail price)
- Advertising—business cards, product literature, sales brochures, classified ads
- Craft co-ops—monthly space rental fee, store commission 5 to 25 percent of retail price, initial contract fee, percentage for credit sales
- Mail order—printing, postage, credit card equipment and processing
- Packaging materials—gift bags and boxes, shipping cartons, tape, ribbon, etc.
- Travel—car expenses/transportation (to and from any selling point), meals and hotels

When you look at the cost of selling you can see why it is especially important to keep your production costs down and to keep a close watch over your expenses.

Multiplying my raw materials by two works well for my products and covers both my overhead and my cost of selling. But most of my products are made with rather expensive materials. The same formula would probably not work as well for products with less expensive parts. You will need to experiment to come up with a basic wholesale price formula that works for you.

Consider the sample product that cost $12.68 in raw materails. That's high. But I like to work with the best fabrics and the best fabrics are expensive, even at a wholesale level.

Multiply the cost of materials by two. That's $25.36. The product takes one hour to make. (When I first started, each piece took 2½ hours.) That's $10.00 labor. Which brings the total to $35.36. I would round it off to $35.00. After years of experimenting, I have found that this price covers all my basic expenses and still leaves me a good profit margin. But if I sold this product through a salesperson, I might have to increase my wholesale price to allow for a 15 to 20 percent commission. Then it might no longer be competitively priced.

When you calculate all the variables and arrive at a selling price, you may decide that you will never be able to sell the product for what the labor and cost of materials warrant and still make a profit. This is a judgment that only you can make. Test your market before giving up on the idea. You may be surprised. Also, reinvestigate your expenses. Maybe there is an area in which you can further economize.

Before giving up on a product idea, ask yourself:

- What do I consider a reasonable profit for this product?
- What can I do to make it more profitable?

- Can I streamline production for more profit?
- Can I buy materials elsewhere at better prices?
- Can I change the product in some way (simplify it) to make it more cost-effective?

If profit margin on a particular product is low, it may be best not to sell that product at a wholesale level unless your sales volume on that item is very high. In that case, purchasing and production costs should go down and profit should go up. The best products for the wholesale market are items you can produce in quantity, offer quantity discounts, cover your expenses, and still make a reasonable profit.

Consider *where* you will be selling your products. More affluent areas can support higher prices than middle- and lower-income communities. If you have justifiably high-priced items, research your selling areas to find out where your market is. Cater to that customer base. If you have moderate- to low-priced products, the less affluent communities may be just what you are looking for.

Effective Pricing—Retail

Usually, your retail price is about twice your wholesale selling price. When you sell wholesale, you sell in quantity and mass produce products, so you have less overhead. The cost of selling is usually less selling wholesale than it is selling retail. But these factors can vary. Use the formula to establish your base wholesale price, then double it for retail selling, but remember that this is just a guide. Experience and selling exposure are the best ways to come up with solid selling prices that work for your products. Be flexible.

If you pay percentages to consignment shops, commissions to salespeople, or entry fees to sell at craft shows, these extra costs should be figured into your retail selling price.

After a few craft shows, if you find that you are not selling, lower your prices a bit at the next show. But make sure you still leave a good profit margin. If that doesn't help, there must be another reason why you are not selling.

If you sell to stores, they usually mark up your product by 100 percent. If you sell a product to them at $35 wholesale, they are likely to sell it for $70 retail. Will your product sell in a store environment for $70? Again, you need to experiment with your particular product. Also, visit some stores and check out pricing for similar items to make sure your prices are competitive.

You may want to set a wholesale price that is slightly higher than 50 percent of your retail price and then offer "quantity price breaks" if the store buys several of a product. You can also set minimum order quantities, but that may only be possible after the product proves successful in a store environment.

The retail selling price for the example product that wholesales for $35 can be anywhere from $35 to $70 (usually closer to $70) depending on your preferred profit margin for that product, your selling expenses, and what the market will bear. This can best be learned by experimenting. I would charge anywhere from $59 to $69 for my products. Will they sell at that price? Yes, they have!

Actually, they have sold for as much as $75, but they took longer to sell at that price. I want to move my inventory in a reasonable period of time. The longer I have an item in stock, the greater the risk of damage. The product will move quickly in the $59 to $69 price range, and I still make a very nice profit on each piece.

Selling in Sets

Having "mix and match" products will definitely give you a competitive edge. Pictured here are intricate 14K gold wire-wrapped bracelets and rings made by Jim Fowler. Jim also sells a wide assortment of pendants and earrings that can be mixed and matched. Offering your customer a chance to purchase a set and not just an isolated piece will go a long way to increase your sales.

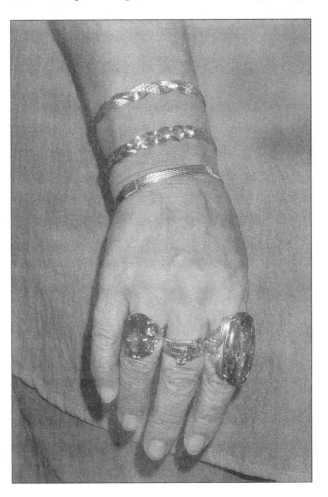

Selling in Sets

Many a potential sale has been clinched or doubled by offering the customer the opportunity to purchase a matching item at a reduced price.

Consider my sample Christmas tree skirt that sells for $69. If I had used my fabric scraps wisely, I may have made any one or more of the following items to complement the tree skirts in my collection and the customer's decor: tree ornaments, a table runner, or a miniature Christmas tree decorated using the fabric remnants from the tree skirt.

I could motivate customers to buy more than one item by slightly reducing the price of a combination of items. For example, I could offer a set of ten matching ornaments for $24. If the customer buys the tree skirt, I could sell the matching ornaments for $20. Instead of making a $69 sale, I could make an $89 sale.

If your products are relatively inexpensive, and the customer is buying a gift item, the cost of one item may not be enough to spend on the gift recipient. The customer may have a predetermined amount in mind. Offering a set could be just what the customer is looking for.

Suppose a customer wants to purchase a set of earrings for $11 as a gift but the price is too far below the $25 she had planned on spending. By offering a necklace or bracelet or ring to match the earrings, you are helping the customer with her shopping and increasing your total sale at the same time! The set should be sold at a slightly lower price than the items would have cost if they were purchased individually.

There are many ways to reduce your costs and increase your sales and profits. As you gain experience, you will discover even more new ideas and innovative ways to save money and subsequently make money. Difficult though it might be, a crafter should always keep the bottom line in sight. Making crafts may be fun, but it won't be fun for long if you cannot make money doing it.

CHAPTER WORKSHEET

This worksheet has three parts. Part One helps you determine how much it will cost to purchase the raw materials for your craft. Part Two helps you develop a production plan. Part Three helps you set the right price for your product by helping you calculate all the expenses associated with producing it.

Purchasing

PRODUCT	RAW MATERIALS NEEDED	RETAIL COST	WHOLE-SALE COST	ACTUAL COST
1) _____	_____	_____	_____	_____
	_____	_____	_____	_____
	_____	_____	_____	_____
	_____	_____	_____	_____
	_____	_____	_____	_____
	_____	_____	_____	_____
	Total HOURS _____	$\times$ \$10.00	=	\$_____
	TOTAL PRODUCT COST			\$_____
2) _____	_____	_____	_____	_____
	_____	_____	_____	_____
	_____	_____	_____	_____
	_____	_____	_____	_____
	_____	_____	_____	_____
	_____	_____	_____	_____
	Total HOURS _____	$\times$ \$10.00	=	\$_____
	TOTAL PRODUCT COST			\$_____
3) _____	_____	_____	_____	_____
	_____	_____	_____	_____
	_____	_____	_____	_____
	_____	_____	_____	_____
	_____	_____	_____	_____
	_____	_____	_____	_____
	Total HOURS _____	$\times$ \$10.00	=	\$_____
	TOTAL PRODUCT COST			\$_____

Production Planning

What product will I make first? _____ How many? _____

second? _____ _____

third? _____ _____

_____ _____

_____ _____

Can I use a graduated product line production schedule?   Yes   No

If so describe it: (See page 88)

_____

_____

_____

_____

_____

Pricing Worksheet

Product					
Materials and Labor					
Plus Overhead					
Plus Cost of Selling					
Equals Total Product Cost					
Wholesale Price					
Retail Price					

CHAPTER SIX

GEARING UP FOR YOUR FIRST SHOW

Now that you have selected a medium and a craft and a product line and know how to buy wholesale supplies and have a good idea how to produce and price your crafts effectively, it's time to explore the avenues for you selling your products. The most obvious place to start is at a craft show. This chapter deals mostly with retail craft shows where you sell directly to customers. This is where most crafters sell their products. Wholesale shows, where you deal with buyers for stores and gift shops, will be dealt with in chapter seven.

Craft shows are a great way to market your products. You get immediate feedback from the people who count most—your customers. At shows, you have access to many different customers, so your products get good exposure.

It may sound like I am partial to craft shows. Well, I am. I love them—from an exhibitor's viewpoint and as a customer. From an exhibitor's viewpoint, shows are social. Each show also seems to teach me something new about crafts. And I am making money at the same time.

If you are ambitious and dedicated, you can make $100 or even $1,000 or more a day at a craft show. Think about it. Even if you participate in only one show a month and you make only $100 at that show, that's $100 (less expenses) you didn't have before. If you participate in two shows a month, that's $200 you didn't have before.

Now think again—if you participated in the same two shows a month and made $300 at each show, you would have an additional $600 in your pocket each month. It could be $1,200 if you did a show every weekend. Wow! Exciting, isn't it?

And where else can you get paid to learn a business you enjoy? Each time you go to a show, you will learn something about your product, about your display, about the market, about selling in general—and you will get paid to learn. And the more you learn, the more you will probably get paid.

Participating in craft shows will help you:

- get to know your customer
- learn how marketable your products are
- practice your marketing and sales techniques
- learn about the crafts market itself
- find out about the competition
- get to see craftsmanship at its finest
- learn a lot about yourself

The customers will let you know if you have a desirable product. They will tell you if your prices are reasonable, if you have chosen the right colors, if you have the right size product. A craft show is a valuable source of information for a new crafter. It is also "trial by fire." Finding the right show, being accepted at the show of your choice, and being adequately prepared to participate in that show are the focal points of this chapter.

The Process—Finding and Scheduling Shows

Finding craft shows in your area should be relatively easy. With a few telephone calls and a few inquiries here and there, you should be able to zoom in on at least a few. Also, you should have been visiting some shows while you were in your research and production stages, so you may already have gathered some craft show information along the way. The best ways to find a craft show in your area are to:

- Ask other crafters about local shows and trade publications that carry show listings
- Inquire at your local craft supplier
- Check newspapers and local events calendars for craft show listings
- Call the Chamber of Commerce in your area for the name of local show promoters

- Check with your local tourism bureau for events that include crafts
- Check the crafters' bulletin boards on the Internet

There are also many regional publications of craft show listings, craft guilds, and crafter information. Here are just a few publications to start you off on the right foot:

The Crafts Report	*The Craft Digest*	*Sunshine Artists*
700 Orange St.	P.O. Box 1245	1700 Sunset Dr.
Wilmington DE 19801	Torrington CT 06790	Longwood FL 32750

The Crafts Fair Guide	*Where It's At*	*SAC*
P.O. Box 5508	7204 Bucknell Dr.	P.O. Box 159
Mill Valley CA 94942	Austin TX 78723	Bogalusa LA 70429

Contact the ones closest to you to start. Each of these publications lists hundreds of craft shows, both local and in other states.

Start by planning to participate in only one show a month if you are doing this on a part-time basis. Then you won't be pressed for time or inventory. If that's not enough, or if you are doing this as a full-time business, plan for one show every other weekend. This should keep you very busy but still give you time to produce inventory as you need it.

If you are really ambitious, and need the money, you can even schedule a show for every weekend, but don't schedule two shows on the same weekend. If you are successful at the first one, you may not have enough inventory to sell at the second one, a potentially embarassing situation. Should you cancel the second show or go anyway with almost no inventory? A good question. If you cancel the second show, the promoter might consider you unreliable and hesitate to accept your applications for future shows. On the other hand, the promoter of the second show would not be pleased to have you arrive with a near-empty display.

Scheduling too many shows can be a time management problem. The more shows you participate in, the more inventory you will need. And, therefore, the more time you will need for production. Space your shows far enough apart to give yourself time to replenish your stock.

I recommend you schedule only one-day shows in the beginning. Two-day and three-day events require a lot of inventory. Even after a one-day show, a crafter can experience "craft show coma." Once you get home from the show and unload your car and store your stock, you will be very tired.

When to Schedule Your Shows

I don't think that a show promoter alive would schedule a January craft show—no crafters would apply to one. First of all, your customers have no money to buy anything, including crafts. They are still getting over the holiday shock to their pocketbooks and paying off their charge card bills. The weather in many areas is also very unpredictable.

Crafters do use the month of January to set up their show schedules for the coming year. This is the month to call promoters for applications, to apply to shows, and to recharge your batteries for the spring show season. Some crafters work on new product ideas and prototypes in January. Others just sit back and relax.

For most crafters, September to December is the most profitable selling season. (Most retailers make half their year's profit during this season.) But don't let that limit you. Though your greatest sales and most active shows will probably be during that holiday season, don't wait until fall to begin selling. Exposure is very important. Get started as early as possible. Fine-tune your new products, work out all the "bugs," test market them, and get them as perfect as possible before your busiest selling season starts.

The contacts that you make year 'round are very important. You develop customers at every show. Some will remember your products. When it comes time to buy— whether for Christmas or otherwise—they may call you and place an order. These customers may see your products at several shows before they decide to buy them. If you compile a mailing list and send them information about the different shows that you will be participating in throughout the year, they may very well follow you from show to show.

It's not only what you actually sell at the show that counts. It's also what you sell as a result of that show. Exposure equals future sales as well as current sales.

Since the fall through the end of the year will probably be your best selling time, you will have more cash than at any other time of year. Don't be tempted to spend it all. What happens in January when you start looking at next year's shows and don't have the money to apply to them? What will happen when you need to restock for the upcoming spring show season and you don't have the money to buy raw materials?

After the first few years, you will know just how much you will need for the shows and to buy the raw materials you will need. So in your first and second year, you should hold back as much money as you can to help carry you through the lean months.

The Process—Application and Selection

Applying to a show is a very big step for the new crafter, but one that shouldn't worry you. In fact, you should be very anxious by now to try out your new products on the public. At this point you should have a reasonable amount of inventory, enough to fill about two tables comfortably. Your basic pricing structure should be in place, though it may change once you have actually tested your market.

Once you have found a promoter, church, school or organization that is sponsoring a craft show, contact them for an application. Keep a supply of postcards on hand that read "Please send information about your craft shows to: (your name, address, etc.)." You might want to include a line about what products you make. You might also want to leave a blank line to fill in the particular show that you are interested in.

If you call, they will probably ask you some questions about your craft and product line. If it is a quality craft show, they will want to make certain that the products you will be selling are handmade by you.

If a show is months away and you are sure you can meet the application deadline, send a postcard or a letter rather than calling. Remember, you are trying to minimize your expenses. If the show is scheduled in the near future, by all means call the promoter to avoid any delays. You don't want to miss out on a show just to save a few dollars.

The promoter is sure to ask for photographs of your product and most likely will also request a picture of your display. Be prepared. They are not looking for professional photos, so you can easily take these photographs yourself. They just want to see what type products you make, what they look like, and, perhaps, what your display looks like. Though your photos do not have to be professional, they should be clear, well centered, in focus and in color. Showcase your best products. Send a display picture that shows all of the other products that you make.

Set up your display and products in your living room or backyard and shoot! Take a few photos of each product in different lighting—some in bright sunlight, some with your camera flash. Take some with a light background, some with a medium background, etc. Select the best photos from the different lighting and setting shots, and always keep a supply of them on hand.

If you don't have room to set up your display, send pictures of your product only. Be sure to bring a camera (and film) to your next show to take a few pictures of your display. Use a 35mm camera for the best results. If you don't own one, borrow one. Most are automatic so you really don't need any special skills to operate them.

Some promoters won't even send you an application or show information until

CRAFT SHOW APPLICATION

One thing is certain in the crafts industry. No two show applications are ever the same—unless they come from the same show promoter. You may never see a show application exactly like this one, but most applications have the same basic information as this sample. There are some key things to note here. This application contains some valuable information and a few "hints" if you know what to look for.

• Juried: Good to hear. At least you know you will be selling alongside crafters selling handmade crafts, not mass-produced products.

• 10′ × 10′ Indoor: That's a standard indoor space size— which is good. They are not skimping or trying to overcrowd the room.

• $45.00: A more than fair price for a show—as long as you sell.

• 15th Annual: Says a lot. Could they (or would they) put on a show for fifteen years in a row that wasn't at least somewhat successful? Probably not. Also, a show that is fifteen years old probably has a steady core of clientele who come back to see the show year after year.

• 75 booth spaces: It's large for a local show. This could be good or it could be bad. The bad news: Though they may limit the crafts by category, there will have to be some duplication of craft. And "75 booth spaces" does not necessarily mean seventy-five crafters. They are telling you how many crafters they can accommodate, *not* necessarily how many will be in attendance. The good news: If the show has been running for fifteen years, and seventy-five is the number of crafters they expect, I would give this show a try.

• White three-sided backdrop: This is very professional and you rarely encounter this amenity at a $45-per-booth show. The backdrop is most likely the "pipe and drape" partitions used at the more expensive shows. At $45 the promoter is not making any money on the crafter's fees, so he must expect to make back his investment on the admission and other features of the show—the food booth, etc. This is actually a good sign. The promoter must expect a lot of people. The crafters are the "draw," not the meal ticket.

• We will advertise: Though I would like them to be a little more specific and tell me in which newspapers and magazines they plan to advertise, at least you know they didn't forget about advertising altogether.

• Five color photographs of your products and display: It is good that they want to see a display photo. Many promoters don't think to ask for this. Usually, when a promoter requests a photo of your display it is to see how professional your display setup is and to help them accommodate your type of display and select the right booth location for you.

PROMOTIONS UNLIMITED presents...

SHOW: "SPRING FESTIVAL"
JURIED CRAFT SHOW

DATE: SUNDAY
APRIL 6, 1994

LOCATION: St. Elizabeth School
324 Meridan Ave.
Lasalle, WI 45678

SPACE SIZE: 10' x 10' Indoor

SHOW FEE: $45.00

SHOW HOURS: 10AM — 4PM (set-up 8 AM)

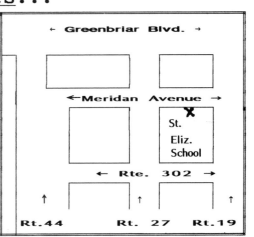

Welcome to St. Elizabeth School's 15th ANNUAL "Spring Festival" Juried Craft Show. Our show will consist of 75 booth spaces filled with the very finest crafts. Each booth has a white three-sided backdrop. Exhibitors are requested to furnish their own floor covering to protect our gym floor. The **deadline** for receipt of applications is **no later than January 6, 1994**. The final jury selections will be made by January 10th. You will be notified immediately after. As always, we will advertise extensively in both local and national newspapers and magazines. Five color photographs — of your products and display — should be submitted. These will be returned to you the day of the show.

———————————————(cut here)———————————————————————————

REGISTRATION FORM

RETURN FORM TO: PROMOTIONS UNLIMITED
P.O. Box 4479   Checks payable to: PROMOTIONS UNLIMITED
Long Hill, WI 12345 (515) 576-4456

ANY INJURY OR DAMAGE TO PERSONS OR PROPERTY CAUSED BY EITHER ITEMS FOR SALE OR DISPLAY, ARE THE SOLE RESPONSIBILITY OF THE CRAFTER AND HIS OR HER REPRESENTATIVE. PROPERTY OWNERS AND/OR AGENTS, AND PROMOTIONS UNLIMITED SHALL BE HELD BLAMELESS FROM ANY LIABILITY THEREOF. I FULLY UNDERSTAND THAT ANY ENTRY FEE IS NON-REFUNDABLE AS SPACE IS BEING RESERVED IN MY NAME. PROMOTIONS UNLIMITED RESERVES THE RIGHT TO ACCEPT/REJECT ANY APPLICATION AT ITS DISCRETION WITHOUT EXPLANATION. ITEMS MUST BE HANDMADE BY **YOU**. YOUR SIGNATURE INDICATES ACCEPTANCE OF ALL TERMS SER FORTH.

_____   _____
        signature   date

☐ PHOTOS ENCLOSED

CRAFTER_____

ADDRESS_____ PHONE:_____

CITY_____ST_____ZIP_____WI TAX ID#_____

PRODUCT LINE_____
ENCLOSE SELF-ADDRESSED, STAMPED, #10 ENVELOPE FOR CONFIRMATION
"SPRING FESTIVAL" — St. Elizabeth School Gym
SUNDAY, April 6, 1994 $45.00 $_____enclosed

they have seen a set of photos of your work. Still others require color slides. Your application may be reviewed by a committee and slides are more convenient for a group to view.

Remember that your photos, slides and introductory package will be your first contact with the show promoter. Present them neatly and in an orderly fashion. First impressions are very important. As they say, you will never get a second chance to make a first impression. If you have to send photos before receiving an application, include a promotional letter to sell yourself and your product.

It is also a good idea to send an autobiography in your package to the show promoter. Tell them some interesting facts about yourself. Describe your products and product line. Brag a little (but not too much). Remember that creative writing course that you took in high school? Now is the time to put it to good use.

You could also include black-and-white photos of yourself, you working on a product, you at your booth, etc. Some promoters use these photos in their publicity campaigns. You might find your picture in the local newspaper!

In summary, a well-prepared crafter ready to participate in a craft show should always have on hand:

- Color product and display photographs and color slides
- Inquiry postcards or form letters to send to show promoters
- An autobiography with interesting facts and history about the crafter
- Copies of newspaper articles or other publicity material about the crafter
- Black-and-white publicity photographs of the craft, the display, the products, and the crafter working at his or her craft

Each show promoter has different criteria for accepting or rejecting exhibitors. Most shows are classified so that applicants have an idea of the type of show before applying. The three basic classifications used to describe a show in any craft show listing magazine are:

- *Open*—Just about any vendor selling any type of product can be accepted provided space is available.
- *Juried*—Only handcrafted items should be accepted. The promoter will probably (but not always) set a limit on the number of booths per craft.
- *Invitation*—Highly selective. Strictly limited to high-quality handcrafted products. Craft categories limited and well defined. You usually have to send your photos, bio, etc., first. If they like what they see, you'll be "invited" to apply.

Open Shows

An open show has the fewest restrictions on vendors and their products. Products at an open show may range from imports (sweaters made in Hungary, toys made in Japan, etc.) to food stuff (spices, nuts, fudge) to "home party" manufactured products to handcrafted items. Depending on who applies to the show, you may find yourself at a show with very few actual crafters. And you could be in competition with vendors of mass-produced products. The "open" label is often used for shows that do not get a good crafter response. They need to fill their spaces with other merchandise and other vendors. Often these shows have titles such as "Holiday Craft and *Gift* Show" so that it covers all the bases.

As a rule, this type of show does not provide a good selling environment for the crafter. How can you compete with inexpensive mass-produced products? Why would you want to? You are selling quality handmade products. You have spent a great deal of time creating your designs and producing your products. You should show them to their best advantage at a show that sells only that type of product.

Juried Shows

The juried show is more selective. With few exceptions, the products at this type of show will be handmade by the seller. They usually require the presence of the actual crafter as the seller and not a "representative." Your photographs will be reviewed by a "jury" of one or more members who will decide whether or not to accept your application and admit your products to their show.

The jury's decision is based on:

- The quality of your work (and sometimes the professionalism of your display)
- The number of other crafters who have applied within your craft category
- Sometimes, how your product relates to the theme of the show

The jury will be selective. They will pick the best—as they perceive it—from each craft category. If your craft category is one for which you know there will be many entries, you should apply very early to be accepted. The package you send to the promoter must sell both you and your products. In some cases, this will make a difference. Jewelry, wood and floral products are always well represented and fill early. When you receive an application for the show, return it immediately. If there is a deadline, make sure you are not late. Sometimes, the jury makes the final choice between two crafters by looking at the postmark on the two show applications. The early-bird postmark usually wins.

If you are the first in your category to enter or if you have an unusual craft or product line, you may have the advantage and a better chance of being accepted. This is why your craft and product line should be as unique as possible. Anything you can do to make your products stand out in a crowd will help you get into the shows you want to attend.

Some shows give an application deadline, then all applications in each category are juried at the same time and what is perceived to be the best of the group is (are) accepted. Other show promoters jury applications as they are received to give applicants time to apply to other shows if they are rejected.

If you are not immediately accepted at a juried show, don't be discouraged. Review your photos and application objectively. Is there anything you can do to make them better before you apply to your next show? You may even want to call the promoter and ask how you can improve your application for the next time. They may offer some valuable insight and you can make adjustments accordingly.

It may just have been a very popular show with lots of applications to choose from. There may be no specific reason why you were rejected. Don't take it to heart. Try again next year if you still want to do the same show. If the show is that popular, it may be worth your while to apply again.

Invitation Shows

This usually means that you have to be invited to *apply* to the show. To be invited you must send a letter describing your work and photographs of your products and display. You must tell and show the committee why you would be a welcome addition to their show. Again, a unique product line and craft have a better chance of being accepted.

I once applied very late to a very popular "invitation only" Christmas show. It was not intentional, I had just heard about the show and it sounded like a good selling environment for my products. So I gave it a try. At first they told me all spaces had been filled. Until I told them what I made. Then they said they always "save" a few spaces for unique product lines. As it turned out, they considered my products unique. I sent them pictures of my products and display, and I was invited to apply.

I was very lucky. But what made the difference was that I had a *unique* product line. Crafters who make Christmas tree skirts are not exactly a dime a dozen. I had such a wide variety of colors, styles and fabrics that I offered something for everyone. That is why I was invited.

But here's another point to consider. The show committee accepted my tree skirts and ornaments *only*. They would not consider any of my Christmas dolls. They had already accepted another crafter who made Christmas dolls. This was acceptable; I wanted to do the show and I had plenty of inventory and variety to easily handle a display of only one or two main products.

Confirmations

Once you have sent your application, the waiting begins. If there is a deadline for applications, you shouldn't expect to hear from the show committee before the deadline date. This could be a problem. If you are not accepted, it may be too late to apply to another show, especially if your craft category is one that usually has many applicants. You may have to settle for a lesser show that still has room for you at the last minute.

Some crafters "double book" shows. If they have applied to a very popular show, they cover themselves by applying to another show on the same date. Then they can choose between the two if they are accepted by both. The downside to this is that you usually have to pay the entry fees for both shows well in advance of the show dates. This could get expensive, and then you have to wait for a refund on the cancelled show.

If you are accepted, the show promoter will send you a letter of acceptance. This should detail all that is expected of you and all that is provided at the show. It should give you information about parking, food availability, loading and unloading, display requirements, setup, breakdown, hotel or motel arrangements and advertising.

Sometimes the confirmation letter includes a layout of the show and the location of your booth. Each show is different. *Read your confirmation carefully*. It may include some requirements not mentioned previously.

For example, one show confirmation I received said I would need a floor covering to protect the school's gym floor. It was two weeks before the show and the floor covering was mandatory. It was an important show, and I did not want to cancel. They suggested plastic sheets but I thought that would be dangerous and people would trip over them. It would also look "tacky." I called a few carpet dealers who told me that for $150 they could supply me with a carpet remnant in the size that I needed. But how would I get the carpet to the show? Where would I store it after the show? It was ten feet long! It was also just too expensive.

Fortunately, I found the solution at a local discount store: a great 8' × 10' indoor/outdoor carpet on sale at $19.95. It folded neatly into a bag the size of a small bed comforter. The carpet looked great with the rest of my display and added to the "homey" look I wanted to achieve. Now I use it whenever I participate in an indoor show, and I use it at outdoor shows too if the ground is wet. I can hose it down after the show and hang it out to dry.

It's best to be prepared for some special requests from your promoter. Be flexible and don't panic. A solution can usually be found.

The Process—At the Show

The show confirmation will tell you when you are expected to arrive at the show. Usually you have two hours before the show opens to set up. Allow plenty of time to get to the show at the designated setup time even if you can set up your display quickly.

Some weekend shows allow for Friday night setup. You don't sell on Friday, you're just allowed to come in and get everything ready for Saturday's show. Take advantage of this opportunity if the promoter offers it and you have the time to do it. You'll really appreciate it Saturday morning when all you have to do is get up, get yourself dressed, and drive to the show. Also, if you have forgotten anything, you will know it Friday night, and you will still have time to bring the forgotten items on Saturday.

If you are very late arriving at the show, the show promoter may give your original space to someone else. When you finally arrive, you might find they have relocated you to a lower-visibility spot. The promoter has every right to do this. He doesn't want a gap in the show line created by your assumed absence. Remember, the promoter is responsible for the success of the *entire* show. It is your job to arrive on time. Be considerate.

Never break down your display and leave before the end of the show. Many veteran crafters will attest to the fact that some of their best sales have been made at the "final hour." I can remember a jewelry crafter named Susan making a $250 sale in the last five minutes of a show.

So even if your sales are slow, stay until the very end. You paid for the space. Make the most of it. Even if other crafters are dismantling their booths, stay set up. Promoters take a very dim view of crafters who leave early.

If you need any special considerations, such as a change in space size (don't abuse the privilege), an earlier setup time, a late arrival, a corner space, a wall space, or any other special requests, notify the promoter well in advance of the show—preferably on your original show application. Don't wait until the night before or the morning of the show.

Space Size

Your display must be flexible. Indoor craft booth spaces range in size from $6' \times 8'$ to $10' \times 10'$ with many combinations in between. I don't apply to a show with a space

Typical Floor Plan—Booth Spaces

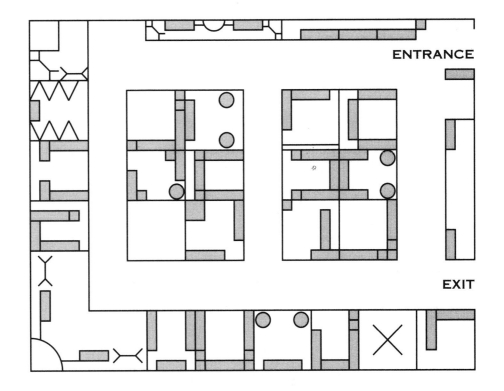

This is a typical floor plan for an 80′×60′ room broken down into twenty-seven 10′×10′ craft booths. You will notice that each booth is different. That's because each crafter positioned his or her display equipment differently. This is to show you there are a lot of different ways to set up the same basic equipment.

Some crafters got square spaces while others got long and narrow spaces (probably at their own request). A long and narrow space can actually be better than a 10′×10′ space if your display can adapt to it. Look at the difference in frontage between the two types of spaces. A long and narrow space can make all of your products readily visible to your customers.

Now let's look at the floor plan itself. Where are the aisles? See if you can track the flow of traffic from the entrance to the exit. Now look at each display setup and follow our key:

• The rectangles represent six-foot tables but they can just as easily represent six-foot racks or a six-foot jewelry case.

• The small squares are card tables. Notice how they fit in nicely anywhere.

• The round symbols stand for pedestals, pedestal tables, and any other small free-standing display accessory such as a circular book rack or ornament display.

• The zig-zag pattern and the "X" pattern represent art display boards for paintings, photography and the like. Art requires a lot of wall space. These suggestions will help an artist make full use of his booth and wall space so that all of his work may be seen.

• The last item, ▸—◂, represents a clothing rack.

Now that you know what all the symbols stand for, which booth configuration would best suit your type of product?

FLOOR PLAN—
TABLE SPACES

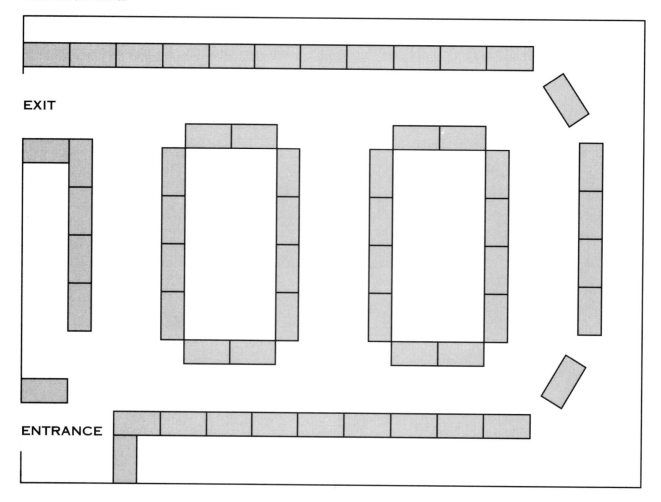

EXIT

ENTRANCE

This is the same 80′ × 60′ room divided into fifty-four table spaces. Can you track the flow of traffic?

size of less than 8′ × 10′. And that is a small space for a display. Any more than 10′ × 10′ is a gift.

If your assigned space has one side longer than the other, confirm with the promoter that the long side will be your frontage. The longer side of your booth space should be the side that faces the aisle and your customers.

Occasionally, usually at school and church fairs, tables are provided. Then you have a choice of bringing your own display or using the tables. If your product is best displayed on a table, that's fine. But if your products are best shown on your own wooden racks or shelves, don't give in to temptation. Bring your own display equipment and decline the convenient offer of the tables. The only products people can buy are the ones they can see.

Other shows give you "table space" only and will provide the tables at a price. Your booth price might be on a "per table" basis. This usually happens at small church and school shows where the show room is not very large. If the room was divided into individual booths, they could only fit a few in the room. So they sell space on a per table basis to fit more vendors into the room and have a variety of crafters.

Odd-shaped spaces, such as long and narrow hall spaces might also work better for your products than a square space. If you have free-standing wood pieces such as cupboards, benches, stools, etc., you might ask the promoter if any "long and narrow" spaces are available. These spaces provide a lot of frontage, so more of your product is visible to customers.

Outdoor spaces are larger than indoor spaces and usually range in size from $10' \times 10'$ to $15' \times 15'$. The additional space is to allow for tents and tent guide ropes. You should be able to adapt your display to fit into any size space. For outdoor shows, it is always wise to make your display so it can fit inside your tent with room for your customers to move about. If it is a nice day, you might want to put part of your display outside the tent, but if the weather turns ugly, you will want to be able to bring it all inside and still have room for customers.

Parking

If space allows, crafters usually have a designated parking area. It is in your best interest to comply. The parking spaces closest to the show should be reserved for customers. You don't want to discourage customers from coming to the show because they couldn't find a place to park!

Even if you are not given a designated parking area, it is in your best interest not to take the nearest and best spots. You may see other crafters parking close to the show. Don't be tempted. If sales are important to you, give your customers every opportunity to come into the show.

Unloading

At some shows you may be asked to unload first, move your car, and then set up. Do this as quickly as possible. The unloading zone may not be large enough to accommodate all the crafters at one time. Be considerate of other crafters and give them space to unload.

Never block the show entrance with your car. Move your car as soon as you can to the designated parking area.

At outdoor shows you may have the added advantage of parking your car behind your booth. This makes life so much easier, especially for a crafter with a large or heavy display and a considerable amount of inventory. And if the weather turns ugly and the show has to be closed, stock damage will be kept to a minimum because you can pack up quickly. This is not the case at all outdoor shows so don't count on it. Just consider yourself lucky when you are allowed to park near your booth.

When You Arrive at the Show

If you received a floor plan in advance, you should be able to find your space with no trouble. The spaces are usually clearly marked. Pay attention to where the aisles and corners are. This will give you an idea of how you should set up your booth and in which direction your booth should face. At most shows, the interior aisles have craft booths that are back to back and the remaining booths are against the far walls. This makes the best use of the room and also keeps the backs of the booths protected since this is where most crafters keep their cash boxes and their extra inventory. If you are confused about how to set up, ask either another crafter or the promoters.

If you did not receive a floor plan, the promoter will most likely greet you as you arrive and show you to your spot. Have her point out the aisles and the flow of traffic. After a while, you will automatically know which markings are for the aisles and which are for the booths. You will be able to figure out the flow of traffic and know which way to set up your booth. But in the beginning, it can be confusing.

Spend your initial time setting up—there will be plenty of time for chitchat later. If you are a new crafter, it will take you longer than you think to set up your display. Your booth should be open and ready for business *before* the show starts. All packing boxes should be neatly concealed and all clutter should be removed from the customers' view.

Once you have set up, take a moment to view your booth from the customer's point of view. Walk down the aisle in the direction of the flow of traffic, as if you were the customer. Are all of your products visible? Does your display look neat, well organized and professional? Is it facing the flow of traffic? Make any necessary adjustments.

The craft show process:
- Prepare for applications—take color photographs of your products and display
- Find a local show
- Write or call the show promoter for an application
- Apply to the show
- Wait for acceptance letter and show confirmation

- Read confirmation for any last-minute changes and to confirm the show rules
- Pack your car the night before the show
- Arrive at the show on time
- Find your space
- Unload your car and set up
- Make any last-minute adjustments to your display and products
- The show begins . . .

Show Etiquette

Crafters should work together to create a pleasant selling environment. Be considerate and congenial to your fellow crafters. Smile, make a joke. You are all in the same boat. Help them if they need your help. They will do the same for you.

Many crafters spend a lot of time worrying about how and what other crafters are selling at a show. Competition is healthy. Your interests will be best served if you take care of your own business. Don't worry about what others are selling. If customers are interested in your product, they will buy it. If they aren't, you can do little to change it at this point.

Preparing to Sell

At whichever show level you choose to start, you will need some basic equipment. I keep all of these things together in one large plastic container—ready to go to any show.

- Sales tax certificate
- Sales tax chart for the area in which you are selling
- Sales receipt book and pens
- "Guest" or mailing list book
- Business cards
- Product labels and price tags
- Self-inking rubber business stamp
- Display equipment and accessories
- Packaging
- Credit card imprint machine and blank debit and credit forms
- Premade signs, extra sign materials and marker
- Display and product repair equipment
- Miscellaneous items—money to make change, a calculator, etc.

SALES TAX CERTIFICATE AND SALES TAX CHART

Your state sales tax certificate should be displayed at your booth while you are selling. Often, state officials visit shows and will ask to see it. If tax is included in your price, you should have a sign at your table. Keep your tax certificate in a plastic case, cover or folder.

If you have checked with the state, and you do not need a tax certificate for the type of product you are selling, you should have a letter from the tax office. Keep that letter with you at the shows. This will eliminate any problems that might arise if a state official questions you. The show promoter might also need to see this.

SALES RECEIPT BOOK

Every customer should be given a sales receipt. Sales receipt books can be purchased at any stationery or office supply store. Make sure yours contains multiple copies—one for your customer and at least one for you. You can also have them imprinted with your business name, address and telephone number to save time. This is definitely worthwhile.

Receipt books also help you keep track of your sales. When you get home from a show, you will have an accurate record of what went on that day. If the show was busy, you may not have a very good idea what you sold or how much. Be specific about your entries if you keep an item-by-item account of your inventory. If you keep just a "category" inventory list such as "earrings—20 pairs," you need not be as specific.

A receipt also gives customers information about you should they wish to reorder. The customer should always be able to contact you if there is a question or problem with the product. You, of course, would want to know if there are any problems. Standing behind your product is very important.

"GUEST" OR MAILING LIST BOOK

An organized crafter will have a "guest book" available for customers to sign if they would like to be included on a mailing list. This is valuable information. Ask anyone who shows an interest in your product, "Would you like to be on our mailing list?" and indicate the book.

When you participate in other shows, you can notify your customers by postcard of the location of the show. They may bring a friend along and make another purchase. Anyone who buys anything from you should definitely sign the guest book, or, if they paid by check, you can save time by adding their name later from the name and address information on the check.

BUSINESS CARDS

Business cards are an important sales tool. They should be simple and complete—your name, your company name, address, telephone number, and product or craft description. If you don't want your address on a business card you should have a post office box number.

Often "scouts" for other shows visit craft shows. If they like your work, they might take your business card and send you an application for their show or call you. That's another reason why a complete address should be included on your business card.

"Picture" business cards are an especially effective sales tool. Let's say you make wood crafts. Almost any photo lab can put color pictures of the various wood products you make on glossy business cards along with your printed information. These are not expensive but they are effective.

Even though a customer might not purchase your product at the show, you can give her your photo business card. At home, she will have a clear picture of your product and can contact you later to order it.

When I participated in an "invitation only" show where the promoter accepted only two of my products, I had photo business cards made up with pictures of my other products on them. And I actually took orders from the photo business cards at the show. At that one show, the photo business cards paid for themselves and more.

PRODUCT LABELS AND PRICE TAGS

Some crafters buy the simple stick-on labels available at most stationery and office supply stores and use them as price tags. Usually, only the price and maybe the product code is written on these small labels. Other crafters use larger labels (or have them printed) and include some business information and an inventory number.

Still others use "tags" connected to the product with string, cord, or colored yarn or thread (a nice touch). These tags may be either purchased plain and just the price added, comercially printed, or imprinted with a rubber stamp design of your "logo" and company name.

The method of tagging you use depends in part on the type of product you sell and the image you wish to portray. Initially, I would keep it neat and simple to keep costs down. You could make your own labels or at least design your own. But this would be time-consuming, and in the early stages of your business, you may want to devote most of your time to building your inventory and other more important considerations.

If you decide to make your own tags, buy some heavy cardstock paper and a rubber stamp with a design that captures the nature of your product line or your company information. The card could be folded in half like a book—your stamp on the cover, your price inside. Punch a hole in the top corner and attach it to your product with string or yarn.

There are many different ways of labeling. Be creative! Nice labels add personality to your products and display. They also show professionalism. And as much information as possible should be included on them without overcrowding.

SELF-INKING RUBBER BUSINESS STAMP

A self-inking rubber business stamp is a handy item that no crafter should be without. It should contain at least your basic information: name, company name, address and telephone number. Self-inking rubber stamps last a very long time and are not expensive. They can be used to endorse checks before depositing, imprint your sales receipts, make business cards (if you run out of them at a show), make product labels and price tags, and stamp envelopes and postcards.

DISPLAY EQUIPMENT AND ACCESSORIES

Your display is a very personal thing and says a lot about you and how you view your crafts. It is also a very important marketing tool. How you showcase your creations can have a direct bearing on sales. And remember, if customers cannot see your products, they cannot buy them.

Your display should be eye-catching and tidy and should show your products to their best advantage. If your product is one that is hung or worn, it should be hung at the show. A shirt lying flat on a table will not catch anyone's eye. A eucalyptus wall wreath will not be shown to its best advantage if it is placed flat on a table. A marionette will just look like a pile of string and wood if it is not "standing." A painting, plaque, floral door decoration or wall clock should be hung or at least displayed in an upright position. Quilts, blankets and tablecloths should be on racks or dowels. Dolls should be on shelves or crates of some kind. And so on.

Make good use of your booth space. To do this, you need to add some height or have some sort of backdrop so that while customers are looking at your products, they can't look across the room to another booth and become more interested in that booth than in yours. A craft show is not a flea market where you sell from an unadorned table. This is a show of high-quality handmade merchandise. You should be proud of your products and you should take the time to display them properly.

If you have done your homework and have a good supply of inventory, you will need a lot of space in which to display it. It can't possibly all fit flat on only one or

SOME STANDARD DISPLAY EQUIPMENT

1. Aluminum folding table

2. Folding table with "skirt"

3. Standard card table

4. Regular director's chair

5. High director's chair—used when you sit behind a high display

6. Folding lattice screens—used for wall hangings, hanging florals, art, etc.

7. Slat shelving unit—great for dolls or small wood items

8. Clothing rack—can be used for clothing or other fabric products

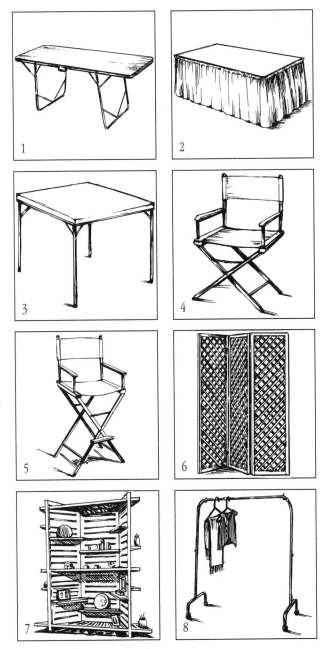

two tables. You will need to build your booth up to accommodate that inventory and bring it to the customer's eye level.

In the beginning you will have to rely on your own creativity to find an effective way to display your products without spending tons of money. But you should always be thinking of how you ultimately want your finished display to look. Go to other craft shows. See how crafters selling similar products have used their booth space. Then come up with a display that's flexible, light and easy to carry, and, most of all, effectively displays your products.

At my first show, I placed all of my Christmas tree skirts on a table. No one saw them, and no one bought them. At the end of the show, I heard someone say "Tree skirts? I didn't see any!" I was too embarrassed to say anything.

Then I enlisted the help of a friend who designed two simple but effective display racks using just wood two-by-fours and wooden dowels to hold the skirts. The display could be easily dismantled and carried. The difference in sales was immediately noticeable too. A customer could walk into my booth, know immediately what I was selling, browse through my inventory and make a selection.

Later on I added a full-size artificial Christmas tree—fully decorated—to my display. A potential customer could actually "try on" tree skirts before making a final selection. And the tree added a nice festive touch not only to my own booth, but to the whole show.

Initially, keep it simple. Just make sure you have a multilevel display. Don't display everything flat on a table. If you use tables, stay away from table covers and skirts in loud patterns. Your table covers should contrast with but not overwhelm your products. Remember that your *product* is on display—not your table covers.

Also, as your product line changes somewhat over time, so will your display. Don't go "display crazy" until you are very sure of the type of products that you will be selling. Your needs will vary depending on your products.

At a craft show, you'll need at least some of the following equipment. It may seem expensive, but you can buy these items one by one over a period of time, and some of them can be made at home by anyone who does woodworking.

Tables and chairs—Sometimes church and school fairs provide them, but most shows do not. You should have your own. A $6' \times 2'$ or $6' \times 3'$ folding table is the norm and can be purchased almost anywhere. Make sure it isn't heavy. You will be carrying it in and out of many shows.

You might also want to consider purchasing a small card table. They are very handy to have. If your space has larger dimensions than you were promised, you can add the card table to give yourself more display area. If the crafter next to you doesn't show up, you might be allowed or requested to expand your display into that booth area so there won't be a gaping hole in the show line. A small card table can also be used as the area where you wrap purchases and write sales receipts.

Your tables should be covered in fabric to the floor. Initially (but not for long), a plain tablecloth or sheet may be used to cut down on expenses. Look at what other crafters use and see how it adds to their displays. The color should complement or contrast your products but never overshadow them.

Also check the fabric for fire-retardancy. Some show promoters allow only fire-retardant materials in displays. You can purchase solutions to apply to your fabrics to make them fire-retardant. After the first few shows, you should have enough money to buy or to make a nice cover and "skirt" for your tables. This looks very professional.

When deciding on what design and fabric you will use to decorate your tables, consider the nature of your products. If you are selling old-fashioned or Victorian products, consider lace overlay for the table cover or skirts or perhaps some sort of washable, durable velvet or an antique-looking piece of tapestry. Also remember that your table coverings need to always look fresh and neat. Make sure that the fabrics you choose are easy-care. Taking them to the dry cleaners every week would be costly.

Your chair should be a folding chair that will fit well in your car. Many crafters use collapsible director's chairs. These work well but any folding chair will do. Some prefer the tall director's chairs because they sit behind their display and need to see over it.

Shelving units, racks, lattice, crates—are all useful items to display your crafts. Obviously, which of these items you use will depend on the type of craft that you make. You can make them or you can buy them from most general merchandise stores and lumber outlets and customize them to your needs. Just remember that you will have to carry and transport all of your display equipment. Display pieces should be modular (able to come apart or fold) and as lightweight as possible. They should be stable and free standing with no outstretched legs for customers to trip over. If you plan to use them for outdoor shows, you will need to secure them so they don't fall over if it is windy. For indoor shows, they need to be stable, so your display won't fall if a customer leans on it, and free standing, because you might not have anything to lean it against.

Tents and tent accessories—You should have a tent for your outdoor shows. Standard tent size is approximately 10' × 10'. Though some of the more professional shows provide huge tents to house their many crafters, most outdoor shows do not.

Veteran crafters have expensive "canopies" for outdoor showing. You will see them when you visit some shows—they are square, with straight sides, and a white peaked roof. These are too expensive for the novice crafter unless you have an abundance of cash and can't find anything else to spend it on. They cost $400 to $700 for the frame and top alone. Side curtains are an additional $250 to $350. Once you start making a profit, you can start saving for one of these.

Initially, you should purchase the gazebo-type tent available at most general merchandise stores. They cost $50 to $75. They aren't quite as sturdy, but they will do just fine for your first outdoor season. They are also much lighter to carry than the canopies. The only negative aspect of these gazebos is their color. Most are made of

TENTS

There are so many different kinds of tents to choose from:

1. Gazebo
2. Dining canopy (not recommended)
3. Professional canopy
4. Dome canopy
5. Protection canopy
6. Pole tent, slant roof
7. Pole tent, flat roof
8. Pole tent, peak roof

striped white/green, white/yellow or white/blue combinations. These colors may distort the colors of your products. Choose the lightest color available.

You may think that a tent is an unnecessary investment, but it can pay for itself at the first show that you do in the rain. If you pay an entry fee for a show and then can't sell your product because it is raining, you have lost that entry fee. It is not refundable.

Many great sales have been made at a rainy craft show. Most outdoor shows are held "rain or shine" and only cancelled in cases of extreme weather. Show promoters expect their crafters to be professional and to be prepared. Don't be a fair-weather crafter.

If possible, you should have side curtains for your tent so the rain cannot get in from the sides. Side curtains for the professional canopies are expensive. Clear (or white) inexpensive, shower curtains work well for this purpose and can be hung from the tent/gazebo/canopy frame with regular shower hooks. Be sure to secure these curtains to the tent at the bottoms and sides so they don't flap in a breeze and upset your product or display. You will need five of them: one each for the back and sides, and two for the front to split into an entrance.

Whatever kind of tent you buy, check the label to be sure it is waterproof and fire-retardant before purchasing. Don't buy the mesh or open-weave tents or you will have to purchase an additional waterproof liner to keep out the rain.

Tent stakes, sand bags, cement blocks, weights—These prevent your display and tent from blowing away in strong winds. Most shows insist that you secure your display. An unsecured tent is somewhat like a kite—it can be picked up and moved quickly by a gust of wind. This is very dangerous. A runaway tent can cause physical harm and product damage—to you or somebody else. Any one or a combination of the above items will save you from disaster. Also be equipped with clothesline, rope and tape, just in case!

PACKAGING

Whatever you do, don't wrap a customer's purchase in old plastic bags that you got from the supermarket. Package it properly.

Boxes are nice, but it is often hard to find the right sizes for all of your products. They are also expensive, and some products just can't be boxed. Nice shopping bags, plain white bags, and clear plastic bags are all OK. Tissue paper is nice. It makes the purchase that much more "special" and shows the customer that you value your product and their patronage.

Just remember not to overdo it. Expensive bags and embossed boxes will decrease your profit. And any clear plastic bag can be turned into a lovely package with a little bit of imagination. Add some colored tissue paper and a yarn bow. It will look fine. Better to keep it simple and neat until your profit allows for more creative packaging.

SIGNS

Don't wait until you get to the show to make the signs you will need for your booth. Here are some suggestions for signs you can prepare in advance:

- "Personal Checks Accepted"

WAYS TO ANCHOR A TENT

Tents are somewhat like kites. They can be easily lifted and carried (even the heaviest of them) in a good gust of wind. The wind doesn't even have to be that strong. Pictured here is equipment that veteran crafters use to anchor tents and tent covers against winds of any kind.

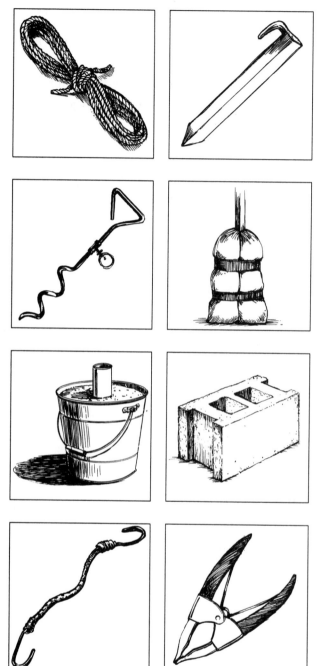

- "We take _____ (Mastercard, Visa, American Express)"
- "We will gladly hold your purchases until you're finished shopping"
- "Free local delivery available"
- "Orders taken today can be delivered by _____ (date)"
- "All sales subject to _____% sales tax."
- "Sales tax is included in all prices"
- "I'll be back in 5 minutes"

Your signs should look as professional as the rest of your display. Print them neatly, either on your computer (if you have one) or by hand, or have someone who knows calligraphy prepare them for you.

Your signs should not be tacked helter-skelter throughout your booth. I keep my signs in inexpensive free-standing lucite paper frames and place them at eye-level throughout my display. They are protected from the weather and remain neat and clean for a very long time.

REPAIR EQUIPMENT

Murphy's Law is almost always in evidence at a craft show. It seems that no matter how hard you try, something always needs fixing. Whether it's your display or a piece of product, you should be prepared. Bring to the show those items that would make it possible for you to repair any minor damage. Obviously, any major product damage will have to be dealt with later on at home.

Here are some items you might need for repairs, depending on what your products and display are made of:

- Tape (cellophane, duct, electrical, masking, two-sided, etc.)
- Nails and hammer, screws and screwdriver
- Safety pins, straight pins, extra thread
- Glue, hot glue, glue gun (with extension cord)
- Extra paint in small pots (don't forget the paint brush)

MISCELLANEOUS ITEMS

Be sure you have everything else you'll need at the time of the sale: cash box, money for change, credit card imprinter and blank debit and credit forms, and a calculator.

Attire

I can't say enough about proper attire. If you are sloppy with your appearance, the customer may assume that the same goes for your product. Funny, but that is often true. Take the time to dress nicely. Remember, you are part of your presentation.

If you sell a product that you can wear, the best way to advertise it is to wear it yourself at the show. It may set you apart from the other vendors. Perhaps an outfit in keeping with your product line will also add to your booth's ambiance. If you do woodworking, why not wear nice overalls? If you have a Victorian product line, add some frills to your outfit. It can be fun to dress up and I've seen it add to sales and put a smile on many a customer's face.

A tidy appearance always leaves a good impression and it will be assumed that your attitude carries over into your work. Dress nicely when you are selling—anywhere.

Attitude

How you act is as important as how you dress. A crafter who complains all the time is never pleasant to deal with. He is a nuisance to other crafters and to potential customers. Greet your customers, maybe hand out a flyer about yourself and your products, and *smile*! It doesn't cost anything and this is supposed to be fun.

Try not to "pounce" on your customers in an effort to be friendly or make a sale. But don't ignore them either. If they have expressed an interest in your product, you might ask, "Which one would you like?" You may want to tell them something about a particular piece that they are looking at, like "That is an original design" or "That stone came from a rare find in South America." This will make the product more valuable to them and will help them justify the purchase.

Never sit back and read a book at a craft show. You are not a disinterested party. You are now both a craftsperson and a salesperson.

There is always something you can do to look busy even if you are not. Rearrange or straighten your products. Fold or unfold them. Play with one of your products if it is a toy. Do something.

In the beginning, you may find it hard to make conversation with your customers. It will take some time and practice before you know exactly what to say.

Initially, you might find that anything you say to a customer makes them walk away. Don't be discouraged. Think of something else to say. Ask about the weather, make a (nice) remark about the child at your customer's side, comment on what she is wearing—anything to break the ice.

It's not as hard as it might seem. It may be a little intimidating in the very beginning, but the "gift of gab" comes sooner or later to every crafter.

Demonstrations

If you have a craft that can be easily demonstrated at a show with no safety factors involved, it is a good idea to do so. People will gather to watch you, and your chances of selling are enhanced. If you wish to demonstrate a potentially hazardous craft (such as glassblowing), get the promoter's permission in advance. Some fire/safety/insurance restrictions may apply.

You might also need to bring a friend to help you sell while you demonstrate, since it is difficult to do both at the same time.

Security

Always keep your money in a safe place at a craft show. An unattended cash box in plain sight is too much of an invitation for some people to resist. You have worked hard for every penny. Don't make it easy for anyone so inclined to relieve you of it.

Many crafters keep their cash well hidden under their tables or under their display. But if you hide it too well, it will be difficult to retrieve when you have to make change. I prefer keeping all of my money in a "fanny pack" securely attached to my waist during the entire show. This way I never have any doubt about where it is.

Never "advertise" the amount of cash that you are carrying. Keep just enough to make change in one pocket. Keep larger bills someplace else—in another compartment of your pouch, in another pocket of your pants. Then when you make change, you won't be taking out a large wad of bills for all to see. And you'll never mistakenly give a customer a twenty-dollar bill as change when they should get a one-dollar bill.

Security is important for your products also. If you have large products, it won't be easy for someone to cart them away unnoticed. But if you have jewelry, miniatures or anything small, there is always a risk that someone just might steal one. This is not to say that crafters are often robbed at shows, but it has been known to happen.

When it does happen, jewelry is often the primary target, because the items are small and easy to take but valuable for their size. If you sell jewelry, take extra precautions. Put your more expensive pieces in a glass- or lucite-covered showcase. Customers can still view your products unattended, but they will need to ask you to take them out if they want a closer look. When you take your more expensive pieces out of the case, only show the customer a few pieces at a time. Return the pieces to the case before taking out any more. Sometimes this alone will discourage would-be thieves.

You could also put your more expensive pieces at the back of your table where they are closer to you. Customers can still see them, but they will have to obviously reach for them if they want a closer look.

If your booth is large, or you have several tables, make sure that you arrange them so you can see everything in your display. If you can't, you might need to add another person to your booth—your spouse, an older child, or a friend or relative— if not to sell, at least to "stand guard." It is difficult to watch an entire booth if you are very busy, or if there are a lot of items to watch.

If most of your inventory consists of medium or large pieces, put the smaller products close to your sales area. This is where (hopefully) you will be most often.

If you are participating in an event that lasts more than one day, take extra precautions. If you have any valuable pieces, don't leave them overnight. If you have jewelry, especially if it is made from precious metals, leave your display set up overnight, but definitely take *all* of your products home each night.

Any product that you leave overnight should be well covered. If prospective thieves can't see it, they probably won't want to steal it. Don't make it easy for someone to walk away with your product.

Customers may not be your only concern. Once in a great while, a crafter takes another crafter's products. If you are participating in a show that is more than one day, make sure the show room is locked when you leave at night. Make it your business to know when the room will be unlocked the next morning, and be there. Then you can be sure that the only products that leave your display are the ones you sold.

A quilter friend of mine, Debbie Barton, had a wonderful idea for protecting her products and display overnight. She purchased several king-size comforter covers ($10 each) that slipped neatly over her quilt racks and covered them on all sides from top to bottom. And it only took her about five minutes to cover her entire display—four large racks filled with quilts! I went out the very next day and bought a set for myself.

Dealing With Customers

Participating in a craft show can be an enlightening experience. You learn a lot about human nature and psychology from your customers. Most are very, very nice. But a few may be a little bit tactless.

Some customers can be quite rude at times. Don't take everything they say to heart. Rise above it. Don't take rejection personally, but do take it seriously.

Many times I hear new crafters complaining that a customer said, "Those are easy to make. I can make them!" If a customer feels that way, it's her prerogative. Let her go home and make it. If you are confident you are selling a quality product at a reasonable price, don't give these comments a second thought.

Pay attention only to the constructive comments made by your customers, those that will help you produce a better product. You are looking for positive input, not some off-the-cuff remark that is made to justify not buying your product.

Occasionally, a customer will insist on haggling over the price of your products as if you were at a flea market. If the customer is buying several pieces, you could offer to pay the sales tax (if it's not already included in your prices), or you could give her a quantity price break of some sort if she's insistent. But if she just wants to buy one piece at a lower price, I would decline. You are devaluing your work. Customers standing nearby will think that they can do the same thing. Pretty soon, you will be cutting your prices for everyone.

Just explain that the price is justified. And that your product will sell at that price either here or somewhere else. But it *will* sell at that price. You should have confidence in your work.

Attending Other Craft Shows

Take time from your busy schedule to visit as many craft shows as possible—small ones and larger ones. Taking a friend with you will give you valuable insight and offer a perspective different from your own.

You will notice immediately the differences in product workmanship, quality of display, and level of professionalism among crafters at different shows. This will give you a good idea of what is expected of you and what the competition looks like.

You'll learn what items sell better than others—at least at that particular show. The wide variety of displays and display equipment will help you put together your own display configuration. Look at the different pricing structures. Do they price in whole numbers or use the $XX.95 method? Is tax included in the prices or does the crafter add it at the time of the sale? Watch how crafters handle customers. Do they talk to them? What do they say? Does it work? Do they ignore the customer? Do they still make a lot of sales?

Evaluating a Craft Show

When you evaluate a show to decide whether or not to do it again, consider the following:

- How much was the entry fee? Did the show justify the amount?
- How was the travel time? Did you have to drive two hours to a mediocre show?
- How many hours did you spend to make the money that you made?
- Were any other expenses involved—hotels, motels, gas, etc.?
- Were there a lot of customers or only a "trickle"?
- Was the booth size adequate?
- Did the other participants also have high-quality products?
- Were you satisfied with your sales?

I know that throughout this book, I have often said "ask another crafter" if a show or other selling situation was good. But remember that these crafters' opinions are relative. When I ask another crafter if a particular show was successful for them, and they say that their sales were "good" or "fair" or "great," I always ask them to be more specific. Some may consider a $100 show (if it was their first one) as a good show. If they had made $300, they might have said it was a great show. For a crafter who has been in the business for a while and is used to selling $800 at a show, a

$500 show would be considered just fair. Still others never say that they had a great show.

Be objective and reasonable in your expectations and don't believe everything you hear. Also consider the source. If you ask a crafter of poorly made products about a show, you could almost predict the answer. And you'll already know the reason why.

There are also crafters who consistently inflate their show success, though I can't imagine why. Others constantly complain about the show they are currently at and tell you how they "sold out" at other shows.

So, you can ask for advice and an evaluation of the show from these crafters, but weigh all the variables and make your own decision about whether to participate in that show or not.

After you participate in a craft show, you will go home, add up how much money you made, and think a lot about what happened at the show. You'll review your mistakes and your successes. You'll probably want to change a few things. Maybe you felt that your prices were too high—or too low. So you'll adjust them for the next show. Perhaps you saw another display that you thought might work well for your products. So you'll redesign your display a little. But the most important thing will be how much money you brought home from the show.

When speaking with new crafters about their success at a show, I find one thing that they all seem to have in common. They are happy if they came home with any money. They are really happy if they earned back their show entry fee. And they are usually thrilled if they came home with $100.

To veteran crafters, any of these situations might be a great disappointment. But new crafters have no way to gauge their success. Since they don't know what a good show is, they often just assume that they had one!

By most industry standards, a retail show is rated as follows. To be an excellent show, the crafter should have sold *more than* ten times the cost of the booth space. To qualify as a good show, the crafter should have sold ten times the cost of the booth. Sales are considered only fair if the crafter only sold six to nine times the entry fee. And a poor show is one where the crafter sold less than six times the entry fee.

So if the show cost $45 to enter, you should have had gross sales as follows to qualify for the ratings listed:

Excellent: $451 or more in sales

Good: $406 to $450 in sales

Fair: $270 to $405

Poor: $0 to $269

This formula neglects some very important criteria, such as the show's duration. Your time is money. If it was a six-hour, one-day show, I guess the formula works well enough. But what if it was a two-day or even a three-day event?

Also, if your product prices are typically in the $3.00 to $7.00 range, your sales would probably not fare well using this formula. At $3.00 each, you would have to sell 151 pieces of product in six hours to have an excellent show rating. That's 50 + pieces an hour, almost a sale a minute! Though it's not impossible, since some sales will be for more than one item, it's not probable either. I don't think that I could even write that fast.

But if you sold 100 pieces you'd be happy, wouldn't you? Yet 100 pieces sold would only be $300 in gross sales. By industry standards, for a retail show, you would have only had fair sales at the show.

The point is, though the crafts industry has tried to create a reasonable yardstick by which to measure success and failure, there can be no such universal formula. If your profit margin was high on the 100 pieces you sold, you should be comfortable with, and, yes, proud of your sales. Only you know how much you spent to make each piece. Only you know how much money you need to make to recoup your expenses and make a good profit. Only you really know when you have had a good show. Don't let someone else tell you when you have had a good show and when you have not. If you were happy with the results, then, for you, it was a good show. And if you keep growing, your next one will be even better.

Use the industry standards if you must as a starting point. You may make more money, you may make less at a show. In the beginning you may consider your show entry fee much the same as the fee for a craft class, only it's an actual selling and marketing class. And $45 is a reasonable price to pay for what you will learn at a craft show. Just make sure that at some point you "graduate" from class.

This is not to say that you shouldn't start making and expecting to make the "big bucks"—or at least the medium bucks. You should expect to. And you will if you keep at it. But be realistic in your expectations, especially in the beginning. Be realistic, but don't give up. You have a lot to learn.

CHAPTER WORKSHEET

The following checklists will help you make your first craft show a success by helping you remember the many important details every crafter needs to do or have.

Applying to a Craft Show

I have the following items ready to send to show promoters:

- Preprinted postcards or form letters of inquiry
- Clear, focused, color photographs of my products and display
- Color slides of my products and display
- A short biography about myself, my experience, my craft and my products
- Copies of newspaper articles or other publicity material about me
- Black-and-white promotional photos of
  - Me at work
  - My products
  - Me *with* my products
  - Me surrounded by my display

What to Bring to the Show

I have carefully packed the following items in one convenient location, ready to take to any show:

- Sales tax certificate and tax rate chart
- Sales receipt book
- Pens
- "Guest" or mailing list book
- Business cards
- Product labels and price tags
- Self-inking rubber business stamp
- Premade signs, extra sign materials and marker
- Repair equipment:

tape	hammer and nails	scissors
safety pins	glue and glue gun	thumbtacks

- Credit card processing equipment

imprint machine	blank charge forms	credit forms
the telephone number to call for credit card approval		

- Product brochures, sales literature and order forms

Other things I need to pack for the show:

Tent equipment:

poles	side curtains	ropes
weights	sandbags	bungee cords
tent stakes	spring clamps	

Display equipment:

shelving units _____ (how many)

tables, coverings and skirt _____ (how many)

lattice _____ (how many)

chairs _____ (how many)

Lights (if you use them):

extra bulbs   heavy-duty extension cords   surge protector (UL listed)

Packaging:

| gift boxes | tissue paper | plastic bags |
| ribbon or yarn | paper bags | |

Petty cash for change:

15 ones, 3 fives, 1 ten should do it

Snacks and drinks

CHAPTER SEVEN

SELLING AT CRAFT SHOWS

There is an art to selling your crafts at any type of show. You will learn best by getting out there and doing it. It takes time and practice and a little effort. Patience and a pleasant disposition are also helpful. But you can do it—you can learn how to sell. And you can learn how to sell well.

Visiting as many shows as possible will help you learn about selling. But nothing will teach you better than actually participating in a show. Watching someone sell is a lot different from doing it yourself.

Once you have decided on a craft and medium and some products to make, you should be able to dedicate effort and time to produce enough inventory so you can at least start selling in about two to three months. Following the advice in this book should move you as quickly as possible to the profit part of the business. That's where selling comes into play. And marketing is the *art* of selling.

Marketing Your Products

Being a successful craftsperson means not only making good products but marketing them effectively. How you set up your display, how you package your products, and how you present them are part of your marketing technique.

It is not only what *you sell, but* how *you sell it that makes the difference. Good marketing techniques will greatly increase your sales.*

Maureen is a crafter who made dolls of storybook and fairy-tale characters. She was getting discouraged because the product just didn't sell and she couldn't figure out why. Here was a cute Little Red Riding Hood doll. When you turned the doll upside down, it turned into the wolf in the fairy tale. It could be turned around again, and the doll would turn into the grandmother in the story—all the storybook characters cleverly incorporated into one doll. Why wouldn't it sell?

After I thought about it a while, I came to the conclusion that the problem was not with the doll itself, but with the *marketing* of the doll. I made a bet with the crafter that I could sell the doll before the day was out. She, of course, was skeptical.

We were at a show in a shopping center. I went into a drugstore in the center and bought the book *Little Red Riding Hood* and placed it with the doll. The crafter increased the price of the doll to include the price of the book. Now she wasn't just selling a doll, she was selling a complete set that included the book and all of the characters in that book.

Not half a day went by before the set was sold. I won the bet and the crafter made the sale. This teaches us something. Marketing is a very important aspect of the business of selling anything, crafts included.

I always suggest to new crafters that, although most of your products should be priced to appeal to the masses, it doesn't hurt to have one special product that is so wonderful that it draws extra attention to your booth, one dramatic piece that will catch the customer's eye. Even if you never sell it, it will pay for itself many times over in customer response and interest.

Sometimes, people need a little encouragement to buy. They need a reason. It is part of your job to give it to them. If you have an expensive product, offer some information on how it was made: the time it took to make it, the process, why it has value. Justify the price so they can justify the purchase.

I have a doll that is a little bit expensive—$48. By explaining the production process—how long the materials were cooked in a dye bath, how long it takes the hand-dyed cotton to dry (two weeks), how long it takes to actually construct the doll— I am telling the customer in a roundabout way that the product is worth the price. Usually, they agree. Here are some features that add value to your work:

- Sign each piece, or just "special" pieces.
- Produce a "limited edition" series.
- Produce a series of collectibles, adding a new design each year.
- Describe the technique or process used to make your products—with pictures, in print, and personally to your customers.
- Show the customer how to use the product, its many applications.
- Demonstrate your technique whenever possible.
- Make your products seem "special" in some way.

One Special Piece

One large and special product, prominently displayed, adds interest to your booth. Customers will want to get a closer look. They will want to touch it. Pictured is a small portion of my display featuring my "one special piece."

When I had a product line of dolls, I gave each one its own personality by adding a written message about each one to my display. For my angel doll I wrote, "It doesn't look like our Sleepy Little Angel will be able to stay awake till Christmas Eve!" For Santa I wrote, "This jolly old fellow will brighten any home for the holidays! St. Nick comes with a burlap sack filled with a special gift for you—holiday scented potpourri!" Since each doll had its own message, customers often spent longer in my booth to read everything that I had written. This gave me more time to spend with them and a better chance to make a sale.

A crafter who sells birdhouses and bird feeders brings a portable tape player to each show and plays a tape of nature sounds and birds singing. She wears her bird-watching outfit, complete with binoculars. It makes you feel like you are outside, standing under a tree. What a nice touch! And it puts customers in the mood to buy her products without her ever saying a word.

Customers seem to go where customers already are. So, if you have three or four customers in your booth, before too long you will probably have five or six, then seven or eight. When customers see other customers interested in your work, they usually become interested too. When they see a small crowd at your booth, they want to be there too, to see what all the fuss is about.

So, here's what crafters sometimes do to help each other if sales are slow at a show. Two of us will walk into another crafter's booth. We'll pick up a product, or ask to see a piece of work and make some comments about it, obviously enjoying it. We'll walk around the booth, ask the crafter questions and touch everything. And before you know it, a few customers will come in to see what all of the fuss is about. Now it's up to the crafter to sell something to them. In a little while, we'll do the same thing for another crafter. Believe it or not, this technique often works very well.

There are many ways you can add interest to your products. There is always a better way to market them. You just need to find what marketing tools and ideas work best for you. Be creative and experiment a little.

Targeting Your Market

You need to have some idea of who you will be selling to. You must be able to recognize your customers when you see them. Ask yourself:

- "What age, sex, size and type of person would buy my products?"
- "Who would they buy them for? Themselves? Their children?"
- "What would they most likely use them for?"
- "What type of environment would best suit my type of product?"
- "Are my products designed/priced for someone at a particular income level?"

This will help you target where you need to sell your products and to whom. If your products are made with expensive decorator fabrics and have high price tags, you certainly wouldn't try to sell them at a craft show in a low-income area. Try to get a mental picture of your customer. When you first designed your products, you must have had some idea of who you would be selling to. Now you need to be more specific. You need to zoom in on your customer.

When you participate in a craft show, take notes about the people who purchased your products, such as how they were dressed, whether they had children with them, what you think their education level was, what their family income might be, where they might live.

Your goal is to formulate a customer profile. Once you know your customers, you can develop more products that will suit them.

Kinds of Craft Shows

Craft shows give you direct contact with prospective buyers and offer immediate feedback about your products from the people who count most—your customers. They give you access to a high concentration of different customers at various age and income levels.

If you have thought of "craft shows" as a limited category, there are many more options than you may have realized. To simplify matters, here are three categories:

Amateur Promoted Shows:

    Church fairs

    School shows

    Nonprofit organization shows

Professional Promoted Shows:

    Retail Shows

    Wholesale shows

Self-Promoted Shows:

    Private corporation shows

    Home party shows (at other people's homes)

    Home shows (in your own home)

It does not make good business sense, especially in the crafts industry, to put all of your eggs in one basket. The more outlets you have for your products, the more consistent your selling will be. You should explore all the selling options available to you and stick with only those that work for you and your product.

Amateur Shows

These shows are organized by a party who is not in the crafts business. You pay them an entry fee and they handle all the preparations, advertising and promotions. These are not professional promoters and they do not promote shows for a living. In most cases, they only promote one or two shows a year.

CHURCH AND SCHOOL FAIRS

Church and school craft fairs are an excellent way to get started. The fees to enter these shows are usually very reasonable—$10 to $45. These shows often rent table space, not booth space. It is a good idea to try a few of these when you're first starting out because the criteria for accepting crafters and their products are usually less demanding than the more professional shows.

Also, you will save expensive entry fees while you're still learning and experimenting. At these shows your display can consist of only one table. At the larger professional shows, such a display would seem meager.

You will also enjoy these small church and school shows more when you're a newcomer since there is less pressure—you won't feel out of place next to some fabulously talented crafter with a fabulous display selling fabulous products and making fabulous sales.

Remember that the organization is putting on the show to raise money for some school or church project or fund. All too often, they consider the crafter's entry fee as their profit and have no incentive to help you make money. Be careful when selecting this type of show. Make sure the organization has a strong commitment to advertising that will bring buyers to the show?

Question the person in charge. What will your entry fees be used for? What kind of an advertising campaign are they planning? How many customers are they expecting? Did they have the show last year? How many customers did they have last year? How many crafters from last year are returning to the show?

Churches and schools are also dependent on parent volunteers to make these events happen, and this volunteer staff is often limited and sometimes unreliable. In the end, they cannot always deliver what they promise. Do your homework before applying.

Customers at these fairs are often school parents or patrons of the church or organization, coming to the show to support the event and the group and to look but not necessarily to buy. We call these people "BLTs"—browsers, lookers and touchers.

Make sure there will be plenty of outside advertising to draw more than just the patrons of the organization. A notice in the church flyer at Sunday service, a paper sent home to school parents, etc., is not enough to support a successful show. Outside interest is very necessary and the organization must convince you that they are committed to drawing customers from the outside and will not be relying on just the patrons of the organization.

Also, if they can't fill their spaces with crafters, they often resort to accepting applications from exhibitors selling imports or other manufactured goods. They may even set up "dollar" and flea market tables—not a good selling environment for a crafter.

Don't consider these shows for long unless they show a commitment to advertising and quality and the show has proven successful for you. Your goal is to turn your craft into dollars. There are sure to be some very successful long-standing church and school shows in your area. Ask local crafters—they will know which ones worked and which ones didn't.

NONPROFIT ORGANIZATION SHOWS

Organizations such as Junior Women's Clubs, Lions Clubs, etc., usually have a better grasp of advertising and commit more money to it. They also have a better grasp of the local free advertising available to nonprofit groups, and they spend their advertising dollars more wisely. Their volunteers seem to show a greater commitment to making the event a success as well. This is not always true so you should again ask some questions before committing yourself.

Professional Shows

These are shows organized, advertised and promoted by people who produce craft shows as a business. Many make their living (at least in part) by producing craft shows. The promoters expect to make a profit on their shows, so they are also in the business of building a good reputation with their crafters and customers. They cannot afford to have too many unsuccessful shows.

RETAIL SHOWS

Retail shows are any shows where you deal with and sell directly to the public. At the larger, more professional retail craft shows advertising is a priority. These promoters are in the craft show business. The professional promoter is constantly searching for popular new areas to hold successful shows, new ways to promote shows, and better ways to draw more customers. Most promoters take their job very seriously. They also produce several shows a year and have greater advertising expertise and resources than a church or school committee that only puts on one or two shows a year.

At retail craft shows, you expect more from your promoter and the promoter expects more from you. They expect you to promote the show to your customers. Often they will send you printed postcards, mailers, flyers, or posters of the event that they expect you to mail to customers on your mailing list or display locally. The promoter and crafters work together to make the show a success. They are integral parts of the same industry.

Competition is keen at these shows. But the profits should be too. Entry fees range from $45 to about $350. As you progress and your sales increase—a sure sign that you and your products are on the right track—you can move to these shows with confidence.

Promoters may hold these shows in a large school gym, hotel ballroom or meeting room, mall, outdoor shopping center, or town green—anywhere they feel will draw a crowd and provide a positive atmosphere for a successful show.

Usually more customers attend these shows, so you will need more stock and a more interesting display. A one-table display of product will not work at this type of show.

Many of the customers will be more discriminating crafts enthusiasts who know quality when they see it. A meager display may turn off prospective buyers even if you have a nice product. Customers like to come to a booth and browse. If it only takes a quick scan for them to view all you have to offer, they may become disinterested and move on.

Some promoters charge an admission fee to the customers. Often it is a way to offset what they paid to rent the room or to supplement advertising and profits. Sometimes it is to help the community or a local charity.

Crafters seem split on the issue of charging admission. Some only participate in shows that do charge admission. Their thinking is that these customers are more serious about buying if they have to pay to get in. Other crafters feel that an admission charge of more than $1 is like asking someone to pay to come into a store. They feel that a large admission charge may turn potential customers away. Only you can decide which is a better selling environment for your products. Personally, I prefer shows that charge admission as long as it is no more than $4.

WHOLESALE SHOWS

Wholesale shows are only for the most advanced crafter who has a large supply of product or who can replenish his or her stock reasonably quickly. Often, the crafter has hired "helpers" to keep up with the orders and sales leads that are generated from this type of show. It becomes a matter of manufacturing more than a matter of crafting.

The entry fees are very high ($250 or more) and the shows often have a waiting list. The high entry fee helps to eliminate the less-than-professional crafter. Your products should be "store quality" or you are wasting your time at a wholesale show.

Sales volume at wholesale shows is generally very high, and although you only show samples of your product line and do not usually sell from stock, you should have plenty of back-up since you will receive quantity orders for quite some time after the show. Business cards alone will not suffice for a wholesale show. You will need a substantial supply of product brochures, preferably in color, and maybe also fabric samples, wood stain samples, etc.

Don't even consider this type of show until you have had substantial success at the smaller shows and have the resources to have quality product literature printed, have the means to increase your inventory fairly quickly, and can afford the hefty entry fee and the price of several nights' stay in a hotel or motel in a major city—plus meals and other personal expenses.

Self-Promoted Shows

You may be surprised to know that you can host your own craft shows. Though a steady diet of only self-produced shows may not bring you profit enough to sustain you, as seasonal shows and as "fill-ins" when you are not committed elsewhere, they can add substantially to your income.

A self-promoted show also offers some flexibility. Shows promoted by someone else are held when their schedule permits. Self-promoted shows can be held when your schedule allows. They are not held on weekends, so they will not interfere with your scheduled craft shows. They can be held almost any day (or night) of the week.

PRIVATE CORPORATION SHOWS

Private corporation shows are usually not scheduled by a company itself. You have to contact them and ask if it's possible for you to arrange a show at their facility. These shows are most often held during some holiday season, but you could initiate one anytime. If you have a large corporation in your area, with over one thousand employees, contact the company and ask if you can do a private showing at their facility. Find out when the employees are paid. You don't want to hold a show the week before payday if employees only get paid once every two weeks.

Usually, the corporation will have you set up in their lobby or cafeteria. The bulk of your sales will be during the employee lunch hours and coffee breaks. You should have a substantial display to do this type of show. If you make a poor showing the first try, they may not give you a second show.

Some corporations take a percentage of your sales for their activities committee or other employee organization. Others charge a flat fee for the space.

Try combining forces with one or more other crafters to offer a greater variety of product. This will add some interest to the show by making it larger and more diversified. You and the other crafters can also split the fee if you are charged a flat rate.

HOME PARTY SHOWS

Home parties are a good way to make local contacts and increase your sales. Many direct selling companies use this method to get their products to the public. There's no reason why you can't do it too.

Home parties are fun, too, especially around the holidays. Have a friend or relative invite their friends and relatives to a private showing of your product line in their home. If it is successful, you could do a show for their relatives and their friends in their homes.

Again, you could combine your efforts with another crafter or two for a larger, more interesting show. If you make jewelry, for example, you might invite another crafter who has a line of clothing or hats that would complement your jewelry. If you do florals, you might want to invite someone with a line of flowerpots, ceramics or baskets for a spring show!

To ensure a successful home party, always:

- Have a free raffle for the guests.
- Accept "catalog" orders (advance sales from your brochure for those who couldn't attend).
- Give the hostess a nice gift—any one of the following.
    - Percentage of sales
    - Dollar bonus for different sales levels reached
    - Special (*large*) product gift
    - Dollars credit toward purchasing her own choices

Sales may be made from stock or you could take orders. Delivery can be made directly to the hostess who will then deliver the products to the customers. Payment should be made at the show.

HOME SHOWS

You may even consider having seasonal showings in your own home to boost your sales and give yourself added exposure. You could open up your home perhaps one day a week. If you have a separate room or showroom for your products, this would work nicely. Note: You may have to check with your local zoning board about a permit if you become *too* successful.

As you gain regular customers and increase your mailing list, home parties become more feasible. Invite your friends, relatives, their friends and relatives, and the customers on your mailing list. Give specific hours and days so that you will be prepared and not have customers calling and coming in at all hours. It is always a nice touch to build your show around a holiday, season or occasion and consistently plan to hold the event at the same time each year.

Advertise in the local newspaper. But have potential customers call you first for an invitation. This way you will not be overwhelmed by the response. And you will then have their names and addresses to add to your mailing list. Send out invitations and offer simple refreshments and quiet music. Your customers will look forward to these "private showings." You might mention in your invitations that you are introducing new products or that you have expanded your product line. This will add a note of excitement and curiosity. Have a prize drawing at each show.

Specialty Shows

Don't limit yourself to craft shows only. Your type of craft may very well fit in nicely at some specialty shows. If you make photo albums covered in animal prints for photos of the family pet, or if you make ceramic pins of different breeds of dogs and cats, consider taking a booth at a cat show or dog show.

If you make wooden furniture and shelving, consider applying to a "home show." If you make sports clocks or other sports items, consider a sports memorabilia show. If you make airplanes, cars, trucks or trains, you might want to participate in a toy show. Or you could participate in a hobby show and sell your products in unfinished or "kit" form.

Be on the lookout for other crafters who have products that would fit in with yours at these specialty shows, so you can share the cost of the booth space and reduce expenses.

A Word About Flea Markets

Flea markets are not especially good places to sell your crafts. Many new crafters have tried and been disappointed. Usually, people who go to flea markets are looking for bargains. They want to buy things cheap. Crafts are not cheap. If yours are, you are doing something wrong.

Occasionally an area may have an upscale flea market that includes high-end antiques and collectibles. You may want to try it and see if your products will sell. The fees are usually reasonable ($10 to $45), so if it doesn't work you will not lose a lot of money. If it does work, that's great!

Standard of Quality

A customer who is dissatisfied with your product—for any reason—should be able to return the product for exchange, repair or refund. Whatever happens, you should never argue with your customer about why the item is being returned. You may *ask*, but never argue. Even if you have to "unjustly" rectify a problem, it is better to do so with a smile. In the end, you will gain more in sales and loyal customers than you will lose in dollars. Good public relations go a long way to enhancing your reputation.

If, for some reason, your policy is "exchange only/no refund," be sure this policy is made clear to the customer before or at the time of purchase. The only time that I might consider a no-refund policy is on a custom order, if I had met the customer's needs and she had simply changed her mind. In a situation like this the materials would probably have been expensive and special ordered for that customer. Even so, if I thought the product would sell to someone else, I would refund just for the sake of public relations.

Crafters wear many hats. They are, to some extent manufacturers, businesspeople and salespeople. The selling aspect is at least as important as the other two. I have seen several crafters who don't have particularly good products, at least nothing special, and they sell like crazy. Why? Because they know what to say and how to exhibit in order to show their products to their best advantage.

If you have taken the time to make good products, you owe it to yourself to use every method you can think of to make sure your products sell. In order to do this you need to:

- Identify which marketing techniques work best for you and your products.
- Know your customer and what they need or will want to buy.
- Select the right type of show for your product.

Selling your crafts calls for as much creativity, and can be just as much fun, as making your crafts.

CHAPTER WORKSHEET

Selling your crafts is an art. This worksheet will help you think of new and better ways of making your products irresistible to your customers.

Marketing

How can I make my products more interesting?

_____

_____

_____

Do I make a product that I can turn into a "limited edition" piece?   Yes   No

Which one? _____   _____

_____   _____

_____   _____

Does my product line lend itself to some sort of "collectibles" series?   Yes   No

Which products? _____   _____

_____   _____

_____   _____

What will I make as my "one large special product" to show my mastery over my craft and to draw customer attention to my booth?

_____

_____

_____

_____

Targeting My Market

Do I know who my customer is? My products are made for: (circle appropriate response)

Senior	Male	Female	Approx. age: _____
Adult	Male	Female	Approx. age: _____
Teenager	Male	Female	Approx. age: _____
Child	Male	Female	Approx. age: _____

Type of household:

Modest income   Middle-class

Upper middle-class   Affluent

Taking the Plunge

I have applied to the following shows:
(enter show title, promoter, date of, show, type of show, date application sent):

My show schedule:

January

_____
_____
_____
_____
_____
_____

February

_____
_____
_____
_____
_____
_____

March

_____
_____
_____
_____
_____
_____

April

_____
_____
_____
_____
_____
_____

May

_____
_____
_____
_____
_____
_____

June

_____
_____
_____
_____
_____
_____

July

_____
_____
_____
_____
_____
_____

August

_____
_____
_____
_____
_____
_____

September

_____
_____
_____
_____
_____
_____

October

_____
_____
_____
_____
_____
_____

November

_____
_____
_____
_____
_____
_____

December

_____
_____
_____
_____
_____
_____

CHAPTER EIGHT

OTHER WAYS TO SELL YOUR CRAFTS

You may have thought that craft shows were your only option for selling your product. This is far from true. There are many avenues for selling your crafts other than shows.

You can have a thriving crafts business without ever participating in any kind of show. You can sell in retail stores, by direct mail or mail-order catalogs.

Displaying your products in a retail store, for example, gives your products greater exposure over a longer period of time. Direct mail and mail-order catalogs seem to be the wave of the 1990s and the way many contemporary consumers choose to shop. Placing ads about your products and services in local newspapers may give you more orders still. Ads in craft magazines may work for your product if it can be sold in "kit" form.

The more channels you have to sell your crafts, the more constant your selling and the more consistent your profit. Multilevel selling will bring you the most profits. So explore the many avenues that are open to you. Try those that you think will work. Keep those that do.

Explore the less costly avenues first. Don't run up large advertising bills until you are sure that your sales can support them. As your profits increase, your advertising budget can increase proportionately.

Here are some of your options:

Friends, Family and Neighbors
Stores
    Selling direct
    On consignment
    Craft co-op stores
    Selling through a salesperson
Direct Mail
    Craft magazines
    Established catalogs
    Your own catalog
    Catalogs of other catalogs
    Direct mail packages
News Media
    Classified ads
    Display ads

Friends, Family, Neighbors

Your friends, family and neighbors may offer you a great network for selling your crafts. If you know people who work for a large corporation or hospital, they may help you launch your crafts business if they are willing to bring your creations to work. Their co-workers may want to order your product. You would be surprised at how many sales can be generated in one building, with one product, through word-of-mouth. You could even offer the seller a commission on each sale.

My friend Arletta worked at a local hospital. I asked her if she would test market a new product for me. She took it to work and I got so many orders that I could hardly keep up—from one friend, selling one product, in one location. Imagine!

So don't ignore the obvious. The people closest to you may be in a good position to help you launch your new business.

Stores

Stores offer great exposure for your products. Merchandise is on display all day, every day, five to seven days a week. And you don't have to be there in person to make a sale. Whether you make direct sales to the stores, sell on consignment, join a co-op, or use a sales representative, selling through retail stores can help you make money.

Choosing a Store

Any store can become your customer if you have a product that complements their inventory. Whenever and wherever you shop, check the merchandise. Would your product look "at home" with the other products on the shelves?

Gift shops are always a good bet. (Don't forget hospital and corporate gift shops!) So are specialty stores. If you sell toys or games, try to market your products to toy shops or educational materials stores. If your item is strictly for Christmas, explore some Christmas shops. The yellow pages of your phone directory will give you access to local names. You could even contact one of the "list" companies and buy a mailing list of, say, all the Christmas shops in the northeast U.S. or all of the gift shops in Texas.

Stores are always looking for interesting new products. Even some of the larger chain stores may be interested if you can meet their requirements and inventory numbers. Be aggressive in pursuing stores, but be sure you can produce the inventory to meet their demands.

You may also be surprised at how many local stores will be willing to sell your products. Though some may reject your offer, you should not give up. More than you might first think will agree to stock your products if your products are store quality and fit in well with the rest of the stock in the store. Until you have some experience dealing directly with stores, don't "load up" on them. Try a few until you get the feel of it and see how much inventory they require and how it all works.

Selling Direct to Stores

Once you find a store where you feel your product would sell well, make an appointment to see the store owner. Prepare your presentation, if you haven't already done so. Approach the owner or manager of the store in a businesslike but congenial manner.

Arrive for your scheduled appointment on time. Bring samples of your products and materials, and photographs of any variations and special orders you have made. This will show your flexibility and will demonstrate your range of talents and mastery of your craft. Listen to the store owner's comments. Be flexible if they want different colors or sizes. Be willing to accommodate any changes that are suggested—if you can. Leave them with any sales literature or brochures you have, even if they have decided not to purchase. They may call you later after they've looked it over in private.

Stores have high rents and high overhead costs so your prices need to be appealing without sacrificing profit. Make sure your wholesale prices are reasonable enough for the store to double for their markup. Offer quantity price breaks for large orders. You should have a set minimum order policy too. Never sell only one piece of a product. Three to five pieces is the minimum.

Some stores will want "exclusives" on your product. (If your products are in their store, they don't want them sold in the store across the street.) Some may want exclusive rights in their *town*. This is OK—if they sell enough. If it's a new customer and you have no other stores in that area, offer exclusive rights on a trial basis only.

Many stores are cautious about doing business with anyone other than their own salespeople or distributors. You should do everything you can to impart a feeling of confidence in you and in your product. Offer a fair return policy.

Getting that first order with a new customer is always the hardest. But if you know that you have a good product that will sell, be persuasive and pleasant but *get that order*. More will follow.

Selling on Consignment

If the store isn't ready to make a commitment to buy your product, you may want to offer them sales on a consignment basis. This means that the store will only pay you when and if your product is sold. Consignment situations can turn into direct sales situations once the product has proven itself. So if this is the only way to get your foot in the door, do it.

When you place items on consignment, you agree to give the store a predetermined commission on the sale—anywhere from 10 percent to 60 percent of your retail price. This will vary, but agree on the percentage before you deliver your product and be sure you can make a profit based on that commission structure.

Add a notation about the consignment percentage to your invoice. Have the owner/manager sign one copy of the receipt for you to keep for your records. These precautions are necessary. Once you have done business with a particular store for a while, your arrangements may change. Whatever arrangements best suit you and the store owner will be worked out in time.

Usually, consignments are paid once a month—like on the 15th of each month—for the previous month's sales. You can call about two weeks after your product is placed with a new store to get some feedback, but don't hound the store to see if your product is selling. Visit only by scheduled appointment.

Many crafters offer a limited stock rotation policy. If a product doesn't sell and has been on the shelf for a while, they offer to exchange it to keep the store's inventory fresh and always moving. Offer to visit once a month to refresh stock, pick up your check, and show new products. Suggest a specific day on which you will return, such as the first Monday of every month—whatever is convenient for the store owner.

If you service several stores, try to schedule your appointments on the same day. This way, you only load up your car once and spend only one day servicing your store customers. The rest of your time can be dedicated to producing more inventory.

Keep your pricing consistent at all stores. The proprietor of one store would not be pleased to walk into another store and find your products at a lower price.

Selling by consignment is time-consuming since you have to keep track of inventory which is "out" but not yet sold. Your inventory will be tied up for a while and you won't have been paid for it. It may also never be sold and in rare cases may be returned damaged or worn. (You might want to include in your agreement that the products must be returned in saleable condition.)

I would like to say, "Only sell on consignment as a last resort," but I know many successful crafters who have a profitable network of stores selling for them on consignment. They visit these stores weekly or monthly, make exchanges on inventory, refresh the stock and display, pick up any repairs and get paid. Then they go merrrily on to their next consignment shop and do the same. If this type of selling suits you, it can be very lucrative.

Above, I mentioned repairs. There will be instances when your product is damaged in the store or when a customer has a problem with the product or breaks it and needs to have it fixed. This is an important service. Again, this is part of selling—stand behind your product. Fix what needs to be fixed, exchange what needs to be exchanged, and refund when necessary—all with a smile. It goes a long way.

Co-op Craft Shops

The latest trend in selling crafts is co-op craft shops. These stores are popping up all over the country. They usually sell only handcrafted merchandise. The crafter signs a contract to display either in a designated area of the store or to have her product mixed in among other crafters' products throughout the store.

The crafter pays a monthly "rent" to cover overhead: salespeople, use of the space, handling, packaging, advertising, etc. This rent is usually based on how much product you have and how much store space is required to display it. In addition to rent, you may also be charged a commission on sales—10 percent or more. Some stores even charge you a fee if the product is purchased by major credit card to offset their processing fees.

The contract might also require you to demonstrate your craft technique periodically, or work in the store occasionally. Read the fine print before signing.

Your lease is usually for a specific period of time, six months to a year. Be very careful. Try to negotiate a trial period of no more than three months unless you're sure that your products will sell. If you have a seasonal product line, such as I do, you may want to request a contract for a more limited period of time—September through December in my case.

If possible, have the store include in your contract *specific* information on the store's advertising policy—where they advertise, how often, and the size of their display ads. Check the local newspapers to see that the advertising schedule is executed. Investigate *before* you sign. Ask for names of other crafters who are in the same co-op and have been for some time. Contact them. Are their crafts selling well at the store? Ask for someone who sells the same type of product that you do or that would appeal to the same customer base. Though "country wood" may not sell well there, "Victorian florals" might have record sales!

Are the proprietors easy to deal with? Flexible? Do they pay on time? How long has the store been in business? These are questions you should ask other crafters.

Since the store's basic operational costs are covered by your rent, they may not be as hungry to sell your products as someone who is selling strictly on commission or consignment.

Many successful crafters sell well in a co-op environment. Some prefer co-op selling to any other selling situation. But not all co-ops are created equal. It is simply a matter of finding the right one, in the right area. Investigate before you sign.

Selling Through a Salesperson

If you would like to devote more of your time to crafting and producing product and would rather leave the legwork to someone else, hire a salesperson (or two, or three, or more!). Perhaps dealing with different store owners and their personalities or spending a day or two in the car doesn't appeal to you. Salespeople know their customers, visit them regularly, and already have a rapport with many different shop owners. They have a network of selling contacts that would take you quite a while to duplicate.

Good salespeople can be objective and give you valuable information on the market and what's selling. They can also give you advice on just how marketable your product really is. They may offer suggestions that you never would have thought of. Most of all, their job is to *sell* your product. For this reason, it may not be easy to contact them. You may have to leave several messages with their answering service before they respond. Remember, they are on the road, where they should be, *selling*!

Finding the right salesperson is probably easier than you think. Visit local gift shops and galleries. If you're out of town, visit shops wherever you are. Since your dealings will be by mail, it doesn't matter where the store or salesperson is located.

If you think your product would sell at a particular store, ask the owner or manager for the name of their salesperson for handcrafted merchandise.

My experience has been that owners are happy to give you this information. Explain that you make products you think would fit in nicely with their merchandise. If a salesperson sells to this store, chances are very good that he has a whole network of similar stores that would be interested in your merchandise.

Selling through a salesperson is a very convenient way to sell wholesale. The salesperson visits the stores, takes orders (armed with photos and/or samples of your product), and sends the orders directly to you. Usually there is a delivery date specified on the order. You ship the merchandise directly to the customer on a COD basis and receive a check within about a week.

Once you have received several orders from a particular store, they may want more liberal payment terms, such as "net 30 days." This means that you send the product via regular shipping (not COD) and they send you a check within thirty days from the date of your invoice. Only consider this if the customer has been buying consistently over a long period of time. You don't want to be in the collections business or have to wait too long for your money. If the store needs more product because it is selling, they won't wait long to pay their bill because they will want to reorder. And, I wouldn't accept any reorders until the account is up-to-date. If there is a past-due balance on the account, don't ship another order until the balance is paid in full.

After you receive your check from the store and it clears the bank, you simply send your salesperson a check for his or her commission (usually 15 percent to 25 percent of the merchandise sale).

Remember to add the total shipping costs to your COD invoice amount. Also, you will need shipping boxes to send your product to the customer. These needn't be anything special, but they should be neat, with your company's name and address clearly visible. This is not to say that you should run out and have shipping boxes printed with your company information. You can buy simple preprinted shipping labels from any office supply store and put them on plain boxes. This is the least expensive way and it will look just fine.

Your salesperson doesn't have to be local. You could service local stores yourself and use several salespeople for out-of-state stores. If you have family and friends living outside your immediate area, have them scout new stores for you. You can call each store to get their salesperson's name and phone number.

Call the salesperson first, and ask if she would accept photos of your products. Ask also what her commission rate is, how many stores she services, what types of stores, and the geographic area in which she makes sales calls. You don't want two salespeople in the same area selling the same products, and I'm sure they wouldn't like that either.

If a salesperson's response is acceptable, make an appointment or send photos and a sample of your products. I put together a small, wallet-size photo album featuring my entire product line and armed my salesperson with one sample of my product.

If a salesperson is not interested because your product wouldn't suit his customers, he may be able to suggest other stores or salespersons that would better suit your product line. If he agrees to represent your work, he will need this photo album, any sales brochures you have, and a sample or two of your products, if they can be reasonably carried in his car. Remember, you are not the only craftsperson he is representing. Do not count on these samples as part of your permanent inventory since they will get used and abused being carried from one store to another.

Orders from your salesperson will become very important to you. Treat her well, pay her as scheduled, and stand behind your product. If a store should return your work, for any reason, accept it graciously, charge the salesperson back for her commission, and go on from there. This has never happened in my experience, but that is not to say that it never does happen.

Some salespeople will also represent you and their other crafters at wholesale shows. Ask the salesperson if this is part of his service, which shows he attends, if there is an additional charge, and what he would need from you in order for you to participate. You will have to pay him a fee, but it will be much cheaper for him to represent you than for you to do the show yourself.

A Store of Your Own

Many successful crafters with extensive product lines eventually opt to open their own retail business. Many wood crafters have opened unfinished furniture shops. Others specialize in custom-built cabinets and furniture. Still others have gone into specialty areas, such as wooden boat repair.

Floral crafters have opened up flower shops. Mixed-media crafters have gone into the gift shop business. Some potters and glassblowers with varied and substantial stock have opened pottery and glass outlets.

Some even continue to participate in the larger retail and wholesale craft shows to supplement their income or to gain added exposure for their new retail venture.

Direct Mail

You may not want any personal one-on-one dealings with customers. Maybe you are the stay-at-home type, but you still like to craft. And you still want to sell your crafts. There are some very good options for running a successful crafts business from home.

Craft Magazines

You can sell your products through ads in crafts magazines. Your local craft store or newsstand is sure to stock a variety of craft magazines. Generally, you should stay away from "how-to-craft" magazines, since their customers are people who want to learn how to make crafts, not buy them. Craft kits, however, sell well in these magazines, so if you sell unfinished pieces or your product can be sold in kit form, the "how-to-craft" magazines may be a good medium for you.

Established Craft Catalogs

There are also several "sampler" craft magazines that feature handcrafted items. You can usually find copies of these at your local craft store.

The customer orders directly from the crafters whose products are pictured and featured in the catalog. The crafter must have "camera-ready" photos of the product to submit to the publisher along with written information describing the product, price and shipping requirements. There is a substantial fee to have your product featured in this type of magazine or catalog.

Information on the publisher is inside the magazine. Call or write, and ask for an advertising package. This will give you all the details, rules, and costs of exhibiting in such a catalog.

If you have an established popular product and no product constraints, this may be a good way to market your product. Make sure your profit margin is large enough to cover all the costs involved in this type of selling: initial fee, packaging, photography (you'll need really good photos). Remember also that you will be selling on a retail level and quite possibly will be selling out-of-state. Research your sales tax liability.

A Catalog of Your Own

If you have acquired a substantial customer following and developed a strong mailing list, you may want to produce your own catalog or brochure. You can also supplement your customer list by trading lists with other crafters and/or buying an already established mailing list from a magazine or list service.

You can buy mailing lists sorted by customer occupation, by household income, by location, etc., from a list service company. You can research these companies at your local library or in the yellow pages of your phone book. Buying a mailing list is expensive. If you are a little patient, you can develop a good one on your own.

Producing your own catalog is very expensive. Anything with four-color printing is expensive. You might try your first catalog in black and white if it won't detract too much from your product. Some first catalogs are even printed with charming drawings of the products instead of actual photos.

You may not have enough different products for a full catalog. In that case, you could join forces with another crafter (or crafters), or you could use a one-page fold-out direct response mailer—much less expensive. Whichever you choose, don't forget to include an order form as part of the package and know your sales tax laws.

It would also help to include a postcard reading something like this: "Send this catalog to a friend. If you have a friend who would like a copy of our catalog, complete this postcard with their name and address and we will be happy to send one to them!" The pyramid effect will go a long way to increase your mailing list without incurring substantial additional expenses.

When producing your first mailer, start conservatively until you see some results. Don't jump into anything elaborate and expensive. It may or may not be worthwhile for you.

Postage will be a large part of your expense. Your local post office can tell you about the different choices in bulk mail permits available to you. These will reduce your postage expense considerably but will require additional work on your part.

Mail may have to be sorted by zip code, banded by zip code and "sacked." Using bulk rate may only be cost-effective for you if you have a number of mailers going to the same zip codes. So if you plan to buy a mailing list, you may want to get one restricted to one particular area to start. Also, there are minimum shipment requirements and there's a fee for the permit. Your local postal representative can advise you. Bring a copy of your mailing list with you, sorted by zip code if possible, and they will be able to offer you sound recommendations and alternatives.

Catalogs of Other Catalogs

If you have produced a professional catalog, and you have had some success with it, you may want to invest in your business further by putting your catalog into a "catalog of catalogs." I'm sure that you have seen them—many large mail-order companies advertise in this sort of publication. But many small businesses also advertise their catalogs in this type of publication.

These catalogs contain hundreds of different catalogs that a customer can order from one source. The catalog publisher charges you a set fee to feature your catalog within its pages. Again, you have to send camera-ready artwork. The customer sends

$1 to $3 (you set the price) to the catalog company to order your catalog. The catalog company then sends you sales leads and you mail your catalog directly to the consumer. Usually, you do not receive the $1 to $3. The catalog company usually keeps this as a processing fee. And you pay about $.50 per sales lead to the catalog company.

You should receive hundreds (often thousands) of sales leads from customers requesting your catalog. You send your catalog directly to the customer. The customer sends their order directly to you and you can add these customers to your regular mailing list and send future catalogs directly to them. There usually is an initial deposit of $1,000 or so to the catalog-of-other-catalogs company.

This option is not for the beginner. Advertising in a catalog of other catalogs should only be considered if you have printed at least 10,000 pieces of your own catalog. You won't believe the response.

Also, your inventory must be substantial at this point. Not that you will get an order for every catalog that you send, but the circulation of these catalogs of other catalogs is in the millions!

Direct Mail Packages

We've all seen these. An envelope comes to your house filled with coupons from local businesses offering services at a discount.

These direct mail packages may offer you a way to advertise in your local community. If you do florals, you might want to put in seasonal advertising for wedding florals or spring bouquets or Christmas wreaths. If your craft is wood, you might want to advertise custom-made furniture. If your specialty is doing drawings of people, you might want to say "We do houseparties—caricatures of your guests! Caricature of guest of honor is free." It will get your name out to the local public, and your information to every household in your area—even those who don't read the local newspaper. I don't know anyone who can resist opening a packet of coupons and reading them!

With direct mail packages you can target a specific town or area in which to advertise. Areas are broken down into zones and you are charged on a per zone basis. the next time you get one of these direct mail packages, give them a call and ask about their rates. (Expect about $400 to $600 per zone.) This is an expensive way to advertise. Only consider this if you have a proven product with a substantial profit margin. Fees like these seriously impact your cost of selling and your bottom line. But this might work especially well if you are planning a home show, because you could target your local community.

News Media

Your local newspaper may be a great source of help in getting the word out about your business. One of the most effective ways to get free publicity in the newspapers is to use a press release. Find out the names of the editors and reporters who handle local news and events. They are always looking for interesting stories about area residents. Send them a press release that tells them something "newsworthy" about your craft-making activities. Invite them to write an article featuring what makes your craft special and different.

Have the best of your work displayed if you get interviewed. You might even get a photograph of you and your work in the local newspaper. You can't buy better (or cheaper) advertising and exposure.

Press Release Basics

At the top of your release, type the words PRESS RELEASE (or NEWS RELEASE if you prefer). Below PRESS RELEASE, in the upper right corner, type your name (or the contact person if it is someone else), the address and phone number. Skip two lines and type the release date (or *For Immediate Release*) and underline it.

Now type double spaced the information you want publicized. Begin with a strong opening sentence that contains the what, where, when and why. Follow that with a more detailed description of what you're doing, emphasizing what makes it newsworthy. Remember, the media is not interested in giving you free publicity, but in giving their audience pertinent and exciting information. Answer the question: "What's in this for the reader?" Conclude with a sentence that mentions or repeats vital facts like show dates or a very brief statement about how to order or get more information.

Skip two lines and end your press release with -30- centered on the line. This is the media's universal code for "the end." Keep it on one page, no more. Newspeople are busy; if you can't sum up your message in one page, it probably won't be used.

Send your release to a daily paper at least a week in advance or two weeks for a weekly paper. If you have good 5″ × 7″ black-and-white photos that illustrate what is newsworthy about your craft activity, send them as well. You probably won't get your photos back, but it is definitely worth sending them for the interest they might generate. And if they are used, the free exposure will be well worth it. If you think the paper might send their own photographer (or a reporter for an interview), allow a little extra time between when you submit your release and the release date.

To learn more about creating really effective press releases, check out the information in Barbara Brabec's book *Homemade Money* (Betterway Books).

Classified Ads

A classified ad in your local (or other) newspaper is a relatively inexpensive way to advertise your product. You won't receive earth-shattering response, but it has been known to produce orders. You could also advertise your home shows this way.

Display Ads

Display ads are larger than classified ads and often use large print and artwork. You may want to place a picture ad with a black-and-white photo or drawing of your product in the newspaper. These ads are much more expensive than classified ads, but they are also more visible since they are put into the body of the newspaper instead of just being listed along with a lot of other classified ads.

These ads are certainly less expensive than a lot of other forms of advertising. You may make some valuable contacts and add names to your customer mailing list without incurring a lot of additional expense.

Where to Go From Here

Often what starts out as a special interest, simple hobby or a small crafts business blossoms into something very different, yet related to your original interests. Many people have started out in the crafts business or simply started experimenting with a medium or a product and this has led them into businesses other than marketing their crafts.

I am one of these people. I started out making crafts. Then I started selling them at craft shows. And I still do. But I have also produced about forty craft shows. It was a natural transition from participating in craft shows to promoting and producing them myself. I sell my products at my own shows as well as at shows produced by other show promoters. So now I have two businesses: producing crafts and producing craft shows. Oh yes, and I am also writing this book about crafts. So, I guess now I have three businesses stemming from my original interests in crafts.

Who knows, a few years from now you might be an expert craftsperson in a particular field and you might write a book about it! You never know.

Many others have started by producing some sort of craft or another and then have combined these talents with other interests. Some don't sell at craft shows at all and they also don't sell to stores. But they are craftspeople nonetheless.

Roger worked with wood. He loved antique wooden boats. He bought one and

ROGER STANDT

Roger Standt of Brookfield, Connecticut, always had a love for fine mahogany speedboats. As a child he watched his older brother take care of his own and other wooden boats moored on nearby Candlewood Lake. And he yearned for a boat of his own.

In 1980, at the ripe old age of fifteen, Roger got his wish. He bought his first mahogany powercraft—a $700 Chris-Craft that was badly in need of restoration. So Roger set to work. It took him one entire winter season to fully restore the boat, but he enjoyed the work and got great satisfaction from seeing the finished results.

Word of what Roger had been doing all winter spread throughout the local boat community, and before too long other wooden boat owners were calling Roger and asking him to repair their boats. No marinas wanted to deal with the labor-intensive restoration of these fine wood crafts, and they just didn't have the expertise necessary to properly restore these boats.

In 1984 Roger, wanting to learn more about these mahogany boats and how to restore them, went to Lake Winnipisaki, New Hampshire, to apprentice with an expert in the field. In 1986 Roger completed his first professional restoration of a customer's boat and got paid for it. In 1988 he officially started a restoration business in the garage of his home. Since many different antique boats are still in the water, Roger saw the need to specialize. He limits his business to

"Mahogany Inboard Powercraft under 30 Feet from 1920 to 1968." And he is still a very busy man.

Totally refurbishing one of these wooden boats takes 1,000 hours. And Roger totally restores one or two boats a winter. In addition to total restorations, Roger also works on about thirty boats a year for general maintenance—varnishing, upholstering, painting bottoms, replacing boards, and doing mechanical work. Roger says, "These boats always need a certain amount of maintenance. That's what keeps me in business."

Roger has turned his hobby into a self-supporting business. He enjoys his work, and his beautiful boats are a tribute to his skill. They are works of art.

rebuilt it. Then someone asked him to help restore another antique boat. So he did. Before too long, Roger was well known as a top craftsman in the antique powerboat restoration industry. He has his own shop and a successful business. He works full time doing what he likes to do—restoring and rebuilding the antique wooden boats that he loves. Though he can't sell this at a crafts show, he still has a thriving crafts business.

Crafting is not a dead-end business. There are many varied opportunities to explore. There are many "side roads" off the main road of crafting.

Crafters who sew may end up designing their own line of clothing. Others with drawing, painting and decorating skills may one day find themselves designing sheets for Wamsutta or making a stamp for the United States Postal Service! (I actually know a crafter who did this.)

Woodworkers may become successful boat builders or custom cabinet makers. A producer of toys may one day find himself selling one of his original toys or games to a major toy manufacturer for mass production and distribution. And he might be able to live on the royalties from that toy for a very long time, if it is popular enough. The possibilities are endless—and astounding!

But for now, take things slow. Start with one craft. Start with one medium. And take the time to learn it well. This alone can be very satisfying. But you never know where you'll go from here. Whichever craft you choose, however you choose to market it, crafting is a wonderful business with many opportunities for exploring and demonstrating your own creativity—in selling and advertising as well as product.

Many crafters live only on the revenues they make from selling their crafts. Many are very successful. Even if you choose to make crafting only a part-time business, it can substantially add to your income.

The key is to minimize your expenses, both money and time, without sacrificing quality. This will maximize your profits. Consider any major expenditure carefully. Do your homework before you make any major monetary commitments. Reevaluate products that take too long to make. Redesign them to cut down on production time.

Select a craft that you enjoy and have fun with it! That is truly what crafting is all about. You can have a successful crafts business from your home. You can have a home-based business that you enjoy. It has already been done by so many. You can do it, too.

CHAPTER WORKSHEET

This worksheet will help you develop a plan of action for finding new outlets for selling your crafts. By making the most of every sales opportunity, you can sell your crafts almost anywhere.

Friends and Family

I have the following family members or friends who could probably sell or at least display my products at work:

Who	*Company*	*Number of* *Employees*
_____	_____	_____
_____	_____	_____
_____	_____	_____
_____	_____	_____

Stores

Selling Direct

The following local stores could be good selling environments for my craft products:

Name	*Location*
_____	_____
_____	_____
_____	_____
_____	_____

- I will visit them and inquire
- I am willing to offer my products on consignment if they will not buy outright
- I will ask them for the name of the salesperson they deal with
- I do not wish to sell direct to any local store

Selling Through a Salesperson

The following stores (not local) would be good selling environments for my crafts:

Name	*Location*
_____	_____

Salesperson: _____

_____	_____

Salesperson: _____

_____	_____

Salesperson: _____

- I would rather sell my crafts myself.

Craft Co-ops

I have found the following craft co-op stores in my area:

_____   _____

_____   _____

- I will contact them and inquire about their contracts and space availability
- I do not wish to join a craft co-op.

Questions I need to ask if I plan to join a co-op:

- What is the duration of your contract? _____
- Do you offer enrollment on a trial basis?   Yes   No
- What are the penalties (if any) for withdrawing early? _____

_____

- Is there an initial fee for joining this co-op?   Yes $_____   No
- Is it a one-time fee?   Yes   No
- Is it an annual fee?   Yes   No
- Will it ever have to be paid again?   Yes   No
- What are the monthly charges? $_____
- What is the space size and location? _____
- Will this be stated in the contract?   Yes   No
- Will I have to demonstrate my craft?   Yes   No
- Is yes, when and how often? _____
- Describe in detail your advertising schedule:
  (ex.: date or day of week, seasonal advertising, name of newspaper, magazine)
- Are you willing to put this in writing?
- I have checked, and the advertising has been executed as promised.

Index

More Great Books
for Creating Beautiful Crafts!

The Complete Book of Silk Painting—Create fabulous fabric art—everything from clothing to pillows to wall hangings. You'll learn every aspect of silk painting in this step-by-step guide, including setting up a workspace, necessary materials and fabrics, and specific silk painting techniques. *#30362/$26.99/128 pages/color throughout*

The Crafts Supply Sourcebook—Turn here to find the materials you need—from specialty tools and the hardest-to-find accessories, to clays, doll parts, patterns, quilting machines and hundreds of other items! Listings organized by area of interest make it quick and easy! *#70253/$16.99/288 pages/25 b&w illus./paperback*

Fabric Sculpture: The Step-By-Step Guide & Showcase—Discover how to transform fabrics into 3-dimensional images. Seven professional fabric sculptors demonstrate projects that illustrate their unique approaches and methods for creating images from fabric. The techniques—covered in easy, step-by-step illustration and instruction—include quilting, thread work, appliqué and soft sculpture. *#30687/$29.99/160 pages/300+ color illus.*

Decorative Wreaths & Garlands—Discover stylish, yet simple to make wreaths and garlands. These twenty original designs use fabrics and fresh and dried flowers to add color and personality to any room, and charm to special occasions. Clear instructions are accompanied by step-by-step photographs to ensure that you create a perfect display every time. *#30696/$19.99/96 pages/175 color illus./paperback*

The Complete Flower Arranging Book—An attractive, up-to-date guide to creating more than 100 beautiful arrangements with fresh and dried flowers, illustrated with step-by-step demonstrations. *#30405/$24.95/192 pages/300+ color illus.*

The Complete Flower Craft Book—Discover techniques for drying fresh flowers and seedheads, creating arrangements to suit all seasons and occasions, making silk flowers, potpourri, bath oil and more! This guide is packed with photographs, tips, and step-by-step instructions to give you a bouquet of ideas and inspiration! *#30589/$24.95/144 pages/275 color illus.*

Jewelry & Accessories: Beautiful Designs to Make and Wear—Discover how to make unique jewelry out of papier mâché, wood, leather, cloth and metals. You'll learn how to create: a hand-painted wooden brooch, a silk-painted hair slide, a paper and copper necklace, and much more! Fully-illustrated with step-by-step instructions. *#30680/$16.99/128 pages/150 color illus./paperback*

The Art of Painting Animals on Rocks—Discover how a dash of paint can turn humble stones into charming "pet rocks." This hands-on easy-to-follow book offers a menagerie of fun—and potentially profitable—stone animal projects. Eleven examples, complete with material list, photos of the finished piece, and patterns will help you create a forest of fawns, rabbits, foxes and other adorable critters. *#30606/$21.99/144 pages/250 color illus./paperback*

Decorative Boxes To Create, Give and Keep—Craft beautiful boxes using techniques including embroidery, stencilling, lacquering, gilding, shellwork, decoupage and many others. Step-by-step instructions and photographs detail every project. *#30638/$15.95/128 pages/color throughout/paperback*

Elegant Ribboncraft—Over 40 ideas for exquisite ribbon-craft—hand-tied bows, floral garlands, ribbon embroidery and more. Various techniques are employed—including folding, pleating, plaiting, weaving, embroidery, patchwork, quilting, appliqué and decoupage. All projects are complete with step-by-step instructions and photographs. *#30697/$16.99/128 pages/130+ color illus.*

Paint Craft—Discover great ideas for enhancing your home, wardrobe and personal items. You'll see how to master the basics of mixing and planning colors, how to print with screen and linoleum to create your own stationery, how to enhance old glassware and pottery pieces with unique patterns and motifs, and much more! *#30678/$16.99/144 pages/200 color illus./paperback*

Nature Craft—Dozens of step-by-step nature craft projects to create, including dried flower garlands, baskets, corn dollies, potpourri and more. Bring the outdoors inside with these wonderful projects crafted with readily available natural materials. *#30531/$14.95/144 pages/200 color illus./paperback*

Paper Craft—Dozens of step-by-step paper craft projects to make, including greeting cards, boxes and desk sets, jewelry and pleated paper blinds. If you have ever worked with or wanted to work with paper you'll enjoy these attractive, fun-to-make projects. *#30530/$16.95/144 pages/200 color illus./paperback*

Everything You Ever Wanted to Know About Fabric Painting—Discover how to create beautiful fabrics! You'll learn how to set up work space, choose materials, plus the ins and outs of tie-dye, screen printing, woodgraining, marbling, cyanotype and more! *#30625/$19.99/128 pages/color throughout/paperback*

The Teddy Bear Sourcebook: For Collectors and Crafters—Discover the most complete treasury of bear information stuffed between covers. You'll turn here whenever you need to find sellers of bear-making supplies, major manufacturers of teddy bears, teddy bear shows, auctions and contests, museums that house teddy bear collections, and much more. *#70294/$18.99/356 pages/202 illus./paperback*

Holiday Fun with Dian Thomas—Discover how to turn mere holiday observances into opportunities to exercise imagination and turn the festivity all the way up. You'll find suggestions for a memorable New Year's celebration, silly April Fool's Day pranks, recipes and ideas for a Labor Day family get-together, creative Christmas giving, and much more! *#70300/$19.99/144 pages/150 color illus./paperback*